Divorce Counseling

Divorce Counseling

A Practical Guide

Marian H. Mowatt

Lexington Books
D.C. Heath and Company/Lexington, Massachusetts/Toronto

Library of Congress Cataloging-in-Publication Data

Mowatt, Marian H.
 Divorce counseling.

 Bibliography: p.
 Includes index.
   1. Divorced people—Counseling of—United States.
 2. Separation (Psychology) I. Title.
 HQ834.M68   1987   362.8'286   86-45898
 ISBN 0-669-14573-4 (alk. paper)
 ISBN 0-669-14598-X (pbk. : alk. paper)

Copyright © 1987 by D.C. Heath and Company

All rights reserved. No part of this publication may be reproduced or transmitted in any form or by any means, electronic or mechanical including photocopy, recording, or any information storage or retrieval system, without permission in writing from the publisher.

Published simultaneously in Canada
Printed in the United States of America
Casebound International Standard Book Number: 0-669-14573-4
Paperbound International Standard Book Number: 0-669-14598-X
Library of Congress Catalog Card Number 86-45898

The paper used in this publication meets the minimum requirements of American National Standard for Information Sciences—Permanence of Paper for Printed Library Materials, ANSI Z39.48-1984. ∞™

87 88 89 90 91 8 7 6 5 4 3 2 1

*To All the Children of Divorce,
Including My Own*

Contents

Preface ix

Acknowledgments xiii

1. Perspectives on Divorce 1
2. To Divorce or Not to Divorce 9
3. The One-Sided Decision 31
4. Practical Problems 45
5. The Stress of Changing Roles 55
6. Dealing with Depression 73
7. Dealing with Rage and Revenge 89
8. Problems with Children 101
9. Counseling for Postdivorce Adjustment and Growth 119
10. Counseling for Remarriage 129
11. Are There Solutions to Dissolution? 143

Appendix: National Organizations 147

Bibliography 151

Index 157

About the Author 161

Preface

Weddings are joyful occasions. Friends and relatives dress in their best, bring presents and good wishes, take photographs, eat cake, and toast the smiling couple on their new life together. Divorce is the opposite event—nobody comes, nobody brings presents, nobody takes pictures, nobody cuts a cake. No one goes into marriage wanting to fail, yet even those who are relieved to be out of a miserable union cannot avoid feeling a deep sense of loss when their dreams of living happily ever after are broken.

Almost half of all marriages in the United States are likely to end in divorce, and the stress and suffering of the divorced surely require as much attention as the problems of the married. In my search through library card catalogs and publishers' announcements I was surprised to find more than sixty books on marital counseling and many on family therapy, whereas I found very few titles pertaining to divorce counseling and therapy. At least seven journals deal with marriage and family problems, yet there is only one journal pertaining to divorce. The *Journal of Divorce* was first published in 1977. Of course, marital counseling books and journals often include sections and articles on divorce, and self-help books for men, women, and children involved in dissolution are published in abundance. Many technical books giving sociological and legal facts about divorce are available, but clinicians who work with divorcing clients need a resource specifically designed to give them practical guidance for counseling on the many problems people face as they go through divorce. I hope *Divorce Counseling: A Practical Guide* will fill that need.

I first learned about the problems of dissolution when I lived through my own divorce. While I gained considerable emotional support and insight from a therapist, I received little assistance for the other myriad problems I faced —where to live, how to rebuild a social life, how to handle my children's reactions to the divorce, how to manage relationships with my in-laws, and how to deal with the confused and distancing attitudes of my married friends. Later as a clinical psychologist I found myself providing divorce counseling.

In my twenty-five years of practice, approximately one-third of my clients have been embroiled in the problems of divorce. Many are referred by attorneys who are prepared to give legal advice but not to cope with their clients' floods of tears and outbursts of rage.

My knowledge of divorce increased when I taught classes on *Divorce— Before and After* at the University of Washington. My students were middle-aged women returning to college and to the job market after many years as homemakers and younger women whose homemaking careers were cut short. All were recently divorced or contemplating divorce. These women needed job-oriented classes, career guidance, and a safe place to work out their practical, social, and emotional problems. They enriched my perspective on divorce, in turn helping me to give my clients greater understanding, and to share my knowledge in workshops for other psychologists. Although no men were included in my divorce classes at that time, I worked for several years with male patients at the Seattle Veterans Administration Medical Center, some hospitalized for serious depression after a traumatic divorce. However, in my practice I have seen more women than men. Men are more likely to feel they must work their problems out on their own. I have seen many couples together in marriage counseling, which often precedes separation, and am aware of the many factors that drive men and women apart.

My knowledge of divorce grew when I began to evaluate couples in custody conflicts for the Family Court of King County, Washington. These angry and vengeful people showed me the extremes of hostility divorce can provoke. Each client presented a picture of innocence and good parenting, describing their spouse's behavior as neglectful and even cruel. These couples rarely sought counseling, but spent hundreds of dollars in lengthy and vindictive court battles that they could not afford.

I have tried to use my varied experiences as thoughtfully as I can in hopes of helping other clinicians who are faced with the kinds of problems that have grown increasingly common in my own practice. To do this, I have first provided background about the history of divorce to place our modern situation in perspective. Next, I have presented ways for counselors to deal with clients who are deciding whether to keep or dissolve their marriages. Subsequent chapters offer specific ways to deal with the practical problems, role changes, and depressed and angry feelings so prominent in the aftermath of a dissolution. I have also discussed ways to guide single parents in coping with their children's problems, and how to help clients find a satisfactory post-divorce life. Since most divorced people remarry, I have included a chapter on appropriate interventions to guide the client toward a second marriage more satisfying than the first. The last chapter describes some community agencies that are responsive to the needs of divorced people, and offers some ways of reducing the number of divorces. A bibliography of books that have been helpful to me, a list of self-help books mostly written by people who have experienced divorce, and a list of books for children affected by divorce and their parents are included at the end of this book.

I use the word *counseling* rather than *therapy* throughout the book since psychotherapy originally referred to the treatment of illness, whereas counseling has generally meant guidance of individuals toward better use of their potentials—a more optimistic connotation. Also, I see divorce counseling as mainly helping people cope with a particular situation, rather than working toward basic personality change, although the latter often results from divorce counseling. I have directed my comments to students and to mental health professionals such as psychiatrists, nurses, psychologists, social workers, and counselors who are trained in personality and development but have had little experience working with clients in dissolution. Without any doubt, in view of the statistics on divorce, they soon will have experience with such clients. For the sake of convenience, I have referred to these clinicians of whatever discipline as *counselors*. Since this book is written in nontechnical language, lay people who do not have access to counseling may find many useful suggestions.

My orientation is eclectic—I use a variety of methods. I believe that all recognized schools of psychotherapy have contributions to make. All are based on the premise that human beings have learned their ways of behaving in the past, are constantly learning in the present, and will continue to learn as long as they live. Thus, I believe that we can unlearn old patterns and relearn more satisfying ones at any age. I move easily from one method to another because I see different approaches as complementary rather than antagonistic, and no one method provides a magic key. Clearly a change in behavior can affect thoughts and feelings; changes in thoughts and perceptions can modify feelings and behavior; changes in feelings can trigger changes in thoughts and actions, all in an endless circling process. Behaviorists and psychodramatists start with behavior; cognitive therapists begin with thoughts and perceptions; client-centered and dynamic therapists usually focus on feelings. No matter where we begin, effective therapy will generally bring about changes in all three areas—thinking, behaving, and feeling.

The examples I use throughout the book are based on people I have counseled and taught, and others I have known. Most are composites of similar cases. All names and identifying information have been changed. I hope this book will give encouragement and guidelines to counselors, and with the help of counselors people will move beyond the pain of divorce to a new and happier phase of their lives.

Acknowledgments

I would like to express my appreciation to all my clients who have shared their experiences with me over the years. This book is about them, and could not have been written without them. And, for her insistence that I could do it, I owe a great deal to Jean Bryant and her workshop, "How to Write a Book." I want to give special thanks to Julianne Seeman, who read every word, edited every paragraph, and taught me so much about writing. I want to extend gratitude to the friends who gave me encouragement, and to my conscientious, tireless typist, Marcella Hook.

1
Perspectives on Divorce

Before counselors begin treating people who are involved in a divorce, we first need to examine our own attitudes toward the breaking up of a marriage. We have grown up in a society where we have formed certain attitudes about marriage and divorce. Our society places high value on marriage as the preferred way of life and views divorce as undesirable. "Living happily ever after" is not just a fairy-tale ending; it is a beautiful real-life goal. Marrying and "settling down" gives definite social status, as though the unmarried are somehow unsettled. Married men often have an edge over the unmarried in business and politics since a wife not only serves as a helpmate, but is also seen as a steadying influence. "Old maid" as a belittling term has not disappeared in favor of the less pejorative "bachelor girl," which in fact implies that she is not yet grown up. None of us is immune to social bias, and some counselors may see their mission as preserving marriages rather than helping couples decide what is best for them. Some counselors—often younger clinicians—may be so impressed with the value of autonomy and personal choice that they may favor divorce. Some modern writers suggest that women's (and men's) liberation includes liberation from marriage (see *The Courage to Divorce*, Gettleman and Markowitz 1974).

Not only are counselors often ambivalent about marriage and divorce, but when they are working with couples they may find themselves favoring either the man or the woman. Women have been treated as the subordinate sex for centuries and have had little power. They have been regarded as silly and superficial, or beautiful and morally superior creatures, and contrarily as the source of all evil and sin. No wonder we can harbor worshipful, contemptuous, pitying, or completely confused attitudes toward the female sex. Reciprocally, men can be viewed as competent, arrogant, powerful and intimidating, or as having one-track minds—that track being sex. No one can grow up without important experiences of men, women, and marriage, which form and color our perceptions. None of us is value-free. Being aware of our values and the ways in which we have learned them can help us approach divorce problems more objectively. Certainly it is helpful for anyone offering treatment for emotional issues to first make their own journey through psychotherapy. Even if counselors feel free from biases and problems, they would do well to know what it is like to sit in the other chair.

Seeing the emotionally charged views that people express about marriage and divorce in a historical perspective is a good way to reduce biases. A brief look at the history of divorce may help us understand how we formed our own attitudes. From the beginning of civilization people have subscribed to the institution of marriage, and as Voltaire remarked, "Divorce is but a few weeks younger in the world than marriage." Nelson Blake in *The Road to Reno* (1962) provides a historical overview of divorce. In the early patriarchal societies of Greece and Rome, marriage was a simple civil contract and it was an easy, private matter for a man to get rid of an unwanted wife. A Jewish husband, under the ancient Mosaic Law, could also divorce his wife since wives were considered the husband's property. Oriental and Middle Eastern civilizations generally followed this patriarchal pattern. Since women did not write in those days I could find no record of how they felt about these inequitable arrangements.

In the early centuries of Christianity in Europe, marriage under the Roman laws continued to be a private arrangement. Wives could divorce but only with their husband's permission. As Christianity grew in power the theologians interpreted the Garden of Eden story to mean that sex was evil and that women were responsible for this sinful activity. Celibacy was therefore the ideal. Sexual intercourse was considered permissible only within marriage and then only for procreation. The church fathers accepted Jesus's edict "What therefore God hath joined together, let no man put asunder" (Matthew 19:6), still part of our traditional marriage ceremony. Another of his sayings, "Whosoever shall put away his wife, except for unchastity, and marries another, commits adultery" (Matthew 19:9), led to confusion and arguments. Did this mean that divorce is forbidden or that it is allowed only for husbands and only if a wife is unchaste? May the innocent remarry? The celibate church fathers argued back and forth for many years. As the Catholic church gained power in Europe, marriage was declared a sacrament rather than a civil contract, to be performed in the church, with witnesses, and it was to be indissoluble. Since adultery was considered worse than divorce marriages could be dissolved on grounds of adultery with no privilege of remarrying. Since husbands exercised almost complete control over their wives, men could of course be granted divorces much more easily than women.

Since people in the Middle Ages, much like ourselves, had many reasons other than adultery for ending unhappy marriages, church members found ways to have their unions annulled so that they could then remarry. The Church was remarkably generous about grounds for annulment, which could be granted if, at the time of the marriage, one member was insane or impotent, had used force or fraud, or if some blood relationship could be found between the parties even if it was remote, or if the marriage had never been consummated. Since annulments had to be paid for, not everyone qualified and abuses became rampant among those who could afford the privilege.

Divorce is an individual matter, but not surprisingly, this very personal action has changed the course of history. For one thing, the need for reasonable ways to dissolve a marriage was in part responsible for the Protestant Reformation. Martin Luther and other reformers were much opposed to the practice of the wealthy obtaining easy annulments. Although Luther believed in the seriousness of the marriage commitment, he wrote that "it was better to allow wicked and unmanageable people to divorce than to condone vexing or murdering each other, or living together in incessant hate, discord and hostility" (*Luther's Works* 1955, pp. 93, 94). Thus, most Protestant sects have allowed divorce on grounds of adultery and desertion, with some including refusal of sexual intercourse and other grounds such as insanity. The innocent party, and in some cases the guilty as well, were allowed to remarry. At the same time, most church groups strongly condemned divorce because of the sanctity of marriage and the importance of the family for children and for society in general. The famous attempt of Henry VIII of England to rid himself of his first wife so that he could marry Anne Bolyn is another instance of divorce changing the course of history. When the King could not get a Papal dispensation to end his marriage he succeeded in having the Archbishop of Canterbury annul the union, which led to the permanent separation of the Church of England from the Roman Catholic Church. This opened the way for less powerful people to end their marriages but after Henry's death the Anglican fathers became more strict about divorce and passed on their traditions to the present-day Episcopal church.

When the poet John Milton was unable to obtain a divorce in 1643, he eloquently expressed his belief that marriage and divorce should be private matters and that incompatibility should be sufficient grounds for ending a marriage. He stated that "it is less a breach of wedlock to part with wise and quiet consent betimes, than still to foil and profane that mystery of joy and union with a polluting sadness and perpetual distemper" (Milton 1847, p. 201). It has taken more than three hundred years for his ideas to be accepted in some localities!

The fiercely independent Puritans who colonized New England rejected the Anglican church's control of family matters, and treated marriage and divorce under the civil laws. But our Pilgrim fathers, being strict and moralistic, considered divorce morally wrong and forbade the guilty party to remarry. People had to petition the legislature for a divorce, and since wives lacked money and were often illiterate, the system was difficult for them. Many unhappy women simply ran away as early newspaper advertisements for missing wives testify. Dissatisfied husbands often took off for the West—divorce laws may have played a part in opening the frontier.

Each colony decided on its own grounds for divorce. When the British government tried to stop this practice, more fuel was added to the resentment that led to the American Revolution—another instance of divorce playing a part in shaping history. After the colonies gained independence people moved westward. Each new state, exhilarated by having won "life, liberty and the pursuit of happiness," proceeded to enact laws with more liberal grounds for divorce including shorter periods of residency and fewer restrictions on remarriage. Imprisonment, intemperance, insanity, and cruelty made their way into the laws as grounds for divorce but usually cruelty had to be extreme or intolerable. Such unsavory grounds may have added to the stigma attached to any divorce yet as early as the end of the eighteenth century the practice of establishing residence in an easy divorce state had begun. Residents of New York state, who had to prove adultery, and South Carolina, where divorce was not permitted until 1949, were among the first to seek migratory divorces. At first, Pennsylvania, then Ohio, Indiana, and Illinois became the "Renos" of the nineteenth century. Further west, shorter residence requirements attracted unhappy Easterners as new western states competed for the divorce business.

As the number of divorces increased during the nineteenth century a stormy debate raged between moralists who saw easy divorce as "free love," which would end family life and the social structure, and more liberal thinkers who insisted that reasonable grounds for ending a marriage were necessary. The conservatives held that marriage must be indissoluble to prevent immorality, while the other side argued that without the remedy of divorce, unhappy marriages would produce adultery, prostitution, and "free love"—all the evils feared by the Victorian equivalent of the Moral Majority. As George Bernard Shaw quipped "Divorce is not the destruction of marriage but the first condition of its maintenance."

Many of the early feminists such as Susan B. Anthony and Elizabeth Cady Stanton, sensitive to the misery of wives chained to "drunkards and tyrants," spoke out loudly in favor of extending the grounds for divorce. The debate continued from lecture platforms and newspaper columns for many years with the more humanitarian view gradually becoming less shocking in the early years of the twentieth century. Social scientists began to view divorce as the result of personal and social problems rather than of sin and immorality.

As the influence of modern psychology spread and the profession of social work was born, marital and premarital counseling began as an attempt to slow down the divorce rate, but were obviously insufficient to reverse the trend. By the 1930s, family courts in many states provided reconciliation counseling and investigations to help settle custody disputes. Unfortunately, some mental health professionals, insisting that immature and neurotic personalities were the root cause of divorce, attached a new psychopathological stigma to marital breakups. Bergler's book *Divorce Won't Help* (1948) is an example of this attitude. Studies of problem children from broken homes added to the guilty onus already placed on divorcing people, who, if no longer "sinful," were considered emotional failures and unfit parents.

This new stigma did not decrease the divorce rate. On the contrary, courts began to interpret old laws more loosely, so that extreme cruelty, for example, came to include mental cruelty, in practice, if not in statutes. This increasing permissiveness plus a growing dissatisfaction with the old adversary procedure, which insisted on guilt and punishment, led in the 1960s to "irremediable breakdown" as a sensible reason for ending a marriage. At that time, ninety-five percent of the divorce petitions in California charged extreme cruelty. Its new Family Law in 1970, designed to do away with this obvious travesty, was the first to initiate no-fault divorce. Dissolution, a less pejorative term, replaced divorce, and soon other states followed suit (see Lynne Halem, *Divorce Reform,* 1980).

By 1986, most of the states had some form of no-fault dissolution and others had achieved a similar goal by including such grounds as incompatibility and irreconcilable differences in their statutes. Even New York, which had clung to adultery as virtually the only grounds for divorce for over a century, finally included separation for one year as grounds for dissolution. This new law, however, required the couple to have at least one counseling session in an attempt at reconciliation. Unfortunately, the old adversary system still prevails in contested custody cases where accusation of immorality is sometimes used to declare a parent "guilty" and unfit for custody or visitation rights. Some states and cities now provide mediation services where such conflicts can be settled in a less hostile setting.

Since divorce is a part of life, social scientists have studied and isolated many facts about it and about the people whose marriages dissolve. George Levinger and Oliver Moles have included summaries of these reports in *Divorce and Separation* (1979). Over a million divorces take place each year in the United States, many involving children, so that divorce affects the lives of at least three million people every year. At the same time, the marriage rate has been increasing, partly because three-quarters of divorced women and five-sixths of divorced men remarry, the majority within three years of their divorce. Samuel Johnson described second marriages as "the triumph of hope over experience." Various studies have shown that second marriages break up at least as often as first marriages—close to fifty percent of the time—with third and fourth marriages even less likely to endure.

The findings are not yet conclusive on couples living and staying together without marrying, and the effect this growing lifestyle of the 1970s and 1980s will have on marriage and divorce rates. Logically, one might expect that living together before marriage would head off incompatible marriages and thus reduce the dissolution rate. But early studies suggest that living together before the wedding is no guarantee of a lasting marriage. Whether the popularity of this lifestyle will reduce the marriage or divorce rate in the long run remains to be seen.

What factors have contributed to the tremendous growth in our divorce rate in the twentieth century? Predictably, marriages of teenagers have the highest rate of dissolution, and if the young wife is pregnant before the wedding, the chances of divorce increase considerably. Seven years after the marriage is the average time for divorce with another peak soon after the birth of the first child, no doubt because the arrival of a third party can upset the one-to-one equilibrium. In recent years more older people are breaking up their marriages, often after twenty-five, thirty, or more years together. This increase in older marriages breaking up is partially attributed to the fact that forty or more years ago people who wanted to separate simply died before taking the step. In the early years of this century women had fewer opportunities to support themselves and the government had not yet taken on the responsibility of supporting husbandless mothers and their children. The thought of having to place children in an orphanage may have deterred many unsatisfied wives from making the break. The liberalization of attitudes and laws as well as the growing climate of self-realization and self-assertion have certainly contributed to the increased divorce rate.

If we know some of the reasons that marriages break up, we also know some of the conditions that tend to keep couples together. Looking at the results of many studies, we find that knowing a partner well for at least a year before marriage, attending church, having a religious wedding ceremony, having parents who have a lasting marriage, and having a network of friends and kin are factors correlated with lasting marriages. Getting to know each other and planning ahead suggest a degree of emotional maturity and ability to postpone gratifications. A supportive group of family and friends lend stability to a marriage, and partners who share the same religion have a better chance of staying together than those of different religions. Partners with no religion have the poorest chance of staying together. Catholic marriages last longer than Protestant ones, and Jewish marriages last longer than either of these groups.

Reports on people with unsuccessful marriages present a somber picture. While the majority of the divorced melt back into the married population, a few, more often men, are found in mental hospitals, where they are overrepresented, that is, out of proportion to their numbers, while married people are underrepresented. The rate of hospitalization for separated people is greater than for divorced. Perhaps the ambiguity of being neither married nor single is more stressful than having a definite status. The proportion of divorced outpatients seen in mental health clinics is also higher than the proportion of married people seen.

One may wonder if the divorce is the cause or the effect of the mental breakdown. Both may be true. Emotionally disturbed people are likely to have a difficult time living with a partner, while some who have been able to cope adequately before, break down under the stress of losing a mate. Many of the hospitalized people are admitted for the first time after the dissolution.

Partly because of emotional stress, divorced people have more automobile accidents than married people, especially in the six months before and after the divorce decree. The rate for fatal motor accidents is three times higher for the divorced, partly because alcoholism is more common in the divorced population. Divorced people also show higher rates of cancer, stroke, and flu, and higher mortality rates in general than married people. Single people, avoiding the stress of both married life and divorce, are least likely to have these illnesses. Divorced individuals are twice as likely as other people to commit suicide or be victims of homicide (see Levinger and Moles).

While the divorces of the rich and prominent make headlines, there are actually more dissolutions among those of lower income and occupational levels, in spite of the often high monetary cost. When a man's income is high, his wife has more to lose if she leaves him. A woman whose husband's income is low may be better off financially on her own. A wealthy man may stay in an unhappy marriage, compensating for it more easily than a poor man through his wider and more interesting career and social opportunities.

Regardless of statistics, divorce can happen to anyone at any stage of life. If we can understand how attitudes toward divorce have ranged from accepting it as a simple civil contract, to the moralistic view of divorce as a sin against society, to the modern but not universal idea of divorce as a necessary remedy for unviable unions, we can be more sensitive to the differing ways in which our clients have learned to react to dissolving a marriage. Aware that over the years divorced people have been labeled as wicked, irresponsible, or emotionally crippled, counselors will understand more easily the emotions that surface from our clients who are struggling through this complex and painful transition.

2
To Divorce or Not to Divorce

Certainly one of the most challenging tasks of a counselor is to help a couple decide whether or not to end their marriage. Since divorce is a major life transition it is not surprising that a couple may take months or years to come to the decision. As Paul Bohannon has pointed out in *Divorce and After* (1971), dissolving a marriage involves not one, but several divorces. First comes the emotional divorce between two people, then the legal divorce involving attorneys and courts and the economic divorce with its financial and property complications. Next comes the community divorce, which means the disruption of social relationships, and if there are children, the parental divorce. Finally comes the psychic divorce, which may not happen until much later when each person has achieved a sense of autonomy and separate identity. With all these hurdles to overcome, it is no wonder that people hesitate a long time before deciding on dissolution.

The well publicized divorces of wealthy people and movie stars may create the impression that those who end their marriages are selfish, irresponsible people, acting hastily and capriciously. And often even those less well known who divorce are criticized for taking the easy way out rather than trying seriously to preserve their families. Couples who blithely separate for trivial reasons rarely turn to clinicians for help nor do those who agree to a mutually satisfactory dissolution.

For couples who seek help then, the situation is quite different. The decision is often drawn out and painful, and usually one person wants the divorce more than the other. To pull out of a commitment, to untangle oneself from a shared life, to leave a familiar routine is like facing the prospect of expensive surgery with no assurance that it will succeed. One moves back and forth between seemingly impossible alternatives—continuing years of unhappiness, or a leap into a thicket of unknown hazards? The more difficult the decision, the more likely these people will come into our consulting rooms.

Probably most of these couples started out with a romantic courtship, a joyful wedding ceremony, and the belief that not only is marriage the best way of life, but *their* marriage will last forever. What becomes of the exiting romance, the wonderful dream of happiness that suffused the wedding, the certainty that love will last "till death do us part"? What happens simply is that romance and marriage turn out to be two different things. Romance is excitement, unpredictability, the magic of being attractive and attracted, the sheer irrational joy of infatuation. As courtship proceeds, the two are on their toes, showing the most loving features of their personalities. When people are in love, positive reinforcement (meaning any behavior leading to positive results will be repeated) richochets back and forth between the two. In my opinion, love is basically mutual positive reinforcement. Or, to use transactional analysis terms, lovers give each other many positive strokes—those signs of recognition and acceptance we crave for our emotional well-being. After lovers' quarrels couples return to the give and take of smiles, physical stroking, attention, praise, gifts, and loving words.

What becomes of all these strokes in a marriage? What is the difference? Marriage, unlike romance, involves long periods of time together so that routines of living and working become predictable and unthrilling. Shared living space, shared relatives, shared social life, and eventually shared children provide endless opportunities for disagreement and conflict as a couple constantly rubs shoulders, compromises, and accommodates to differing habits, attitudes, and priorities. In *Marriage is a Loving Business* (1977), Hauck concisely describes the relationship, comparing it to a business partnership, which in fact it is. But how often do people choose a marriage partner as carefully as they would a business partner, or as cautiously as parents in the past used to pick a financially and socially suitable spouse for their offspring? Romance and the fallacious notion that love conquers all too often prevent couples from deliberating the pros and cons of marriage as long and thoroughly as they may later think through the decision to divorce. In *The Hoax of Romance* (1981), Jo Loudin explored the history of romance and indited it as the enemy rather than the precursor of lasting relationships. Romantic feelings lead people to marry for exciting reasons like sexual attraction and blind them to more important considerations. Because romance and falling in love are such a staple in our folklore of marriage, young people will often unrealistically expect that the fun, the charming manners, and the fascination of dating and courtship will continue forever in spite of a tight budget, a tiny apartment, and daily housework. When the daydream fails to come true, each may begin to blame the other.

In her book *The American Way of Divorce: A Prescription for Change* (1975), Sheila Kessler, a psychologist who has worked extensively with divorce adjustment groups, describes the gradual fading of romance and erosion of the relationship. At first a few disappointments inevitably occur—a husband wants to resume his Friday night bowling league instead of celebrating the end of the work week with his bride or a wife wants to have Sunday dinner every week with her parents. As disappointments recur, resentments grow, criticisms multiply, and the pair may express anger and retaliate more often and more hurtfully. Negative strokes begin to outnumber the positive and the diminishing emotional supplies may lead to detachment and withdrawal. Next, people may seek various escapes such as drinking, concentrating overtime on work, or having an affair. These escapes only escalate the conflicts. Some come into counseling after one of these avenues has created a crisis such as physical violence.

If the disappointments and abuses have wiped out the wish to restore loving behavior no amount of counseling is likely to save the marriage, and counselors need not feel they have failed at their job. Perhaps the majority of couples who come for help have waited until the situation has deteriorated beyond repair. Often their counseling agenda may be a cry for help to break out of the marriage, or an attempt to force the other to change, or a mere gesture to prove to the spouse that "I've tried." When I saw one couple for the first and only time the wife sat rigidly, and her very revealing contribution to the interview was "I told him I'd come, so I'm here." She had already made up her mind to leave her husband. He had to give up the all too common hope that counseling can solve all problems and accept the inevitable dissolution.

What brings confused, unhappy couples to such an impasse? Many reasons beside romantic illusions may play a part. A man and a woman are different beings from the start. Girl babies are generally more placid and responsive to people than boy babies, and parents treat boy babies less gently than girls and encourage more active play. In spite of the movement toward nonsexist childrearing, girls still play with dolls and play house, while boys favor cars and cap pistols. Girls tend to identify with their mothers, and if mother is nurturing, they are likely to take on this trait. Boys, on the other hand, usually want to avoid identifying with mother so they may suppress gentle feelings in favor of a tough, strong facade. I find it is usually the wife who expresses feelings more easily than her husband. This discrepancy can lead to frustration and arguments.

Not only are most women more expressive of feelings than their husbands, but also they are usually more verbally fluent. Girls begin to talk at an earlier age than boys. They tend to excel in language studies in school and enjoy getting together with other girls just to talk. Later, talking with women friends over coffee affords a kind of enjoyment and support that is apparently not as available to men in our society and perhaps not as necessary or enjoyable for them. Rose and Peter are a good example of this difference. After six years of marriage Rose claimed that Peter never talked to her. Frustrated in her attempts to stir up pleasant conversation, Rose finally demanded "Talk to me! Talk to me!" Peter usually responded to this plea with "All right, what do you want me to talk about?" which ended the interchange. In their counseling sessions Rose naturally did most of the talking, not realizing until too late that her desperate insistence only served to alienate Peter. Eventually he decided to leave and look for a less demanding partner. I have heard other men describe their wish just to have their wives in the house with them. Apparently this is as satisfying to some men as sharing conversation is to their wives.

In addition to gender differences, each person comes from a different family group. Understanding the place a man and woman held in their family constellation can throw light on their interactions. The eldest child can be a powerful, privileged person, or a resentful, overworked babysitter for younger siblings. The youngest may be petted and indulged, or ignored as an unwanted nuisance. These feelings about oneself are carried into the marriage. Psychologists have studied the effects of ordinal position on marriage relationships and have postulated that a union between a woman who was the eldest and a man who was the youngest may make a better fit than a marriage of two eldest children, or two youngest children. Attitudes toward brothers and sisters can color one's feelings toward the spouse. A girl's resentful attitude toward her overprivileged brothers, for example, may influence her feelings toward other men. Tom had several sisters whom he found bossy and intrusive, and sought peace by locking himself in his room—a habit his wife could not tolerate when he carried it into their marriage.

Certainly the viability of a marriage is often balanced on the clients' self-acceptance and ability to accept other less than perfect people. Some writers have called these attitudes, learned early in the family, security and trust. Harris (1969) has labeled this ability to accept as *I'm O.K., you're O.K.* Without at least a minimum of acceptance it will be difficult for people to tolerate the stresses of living together and they will lack the flexibility to handle their inevitable frustrations in constructive ways.

The stresses of living together can be troubling even when the two partners share similar economic, social, and educational backgrounds. If they grew up with different educational goals, or learned different moral values, misunderstandings can be compounded. Still more unstable may be a marriage of people from different racial or ethnic groups, or different countries, which can produce conflicts in values and expectations.

Even without such divergences a matter of timing differences may cause conflict. Gail Sheehy in *Passages* (1976) has described women who have stayed home and raised children and who at forty may be ready to consider their own needs. After going to college or finding an interesting job, they begin to enjoy new outside interests, whereas their husbands may grow tired of the hectic business world. At this stage the men may decide to devote more attention to home, wives, and children. Since by this time wives and children are off on their own pursuits, the bad timing can lead to serious disappointments.

All of this background information is important in counseling a couple who is trying to decide on a divorce. Since I make my own appointments I begin to learn about a couple from the first telephone call. The caller is likely to be the one most upset, probably because he or she wants to prevent the divorce. When the couple comes in for the first interview they write down the usual identifying information as well as information regarding birthplace; names and ages of parents, siblings, and children; education and jobs; dates of marriage; and previous psychotherapy. This gives me a framework on which to hang some of the differences in attitudes that emerge in the interviews. At the first session I note how the couple decides which person will talk first. I notice their nonverbal reactions to each other, and how they interrupt and contradict each other. I usually see them separately before the next joint meeting in order to learn more about their personalities and backgrounds and to find out if there are important issues they failed to bring up in the joint interview. For example, Gertrude, age forty, married for twenty years with two children, had been vague about her reasons for wishing to leave Terry, her husband. In the individual session she confessed that she was involved in a serious affair that she intended to continue. Such information, of course, must come out before a satisfactory decision can be made, but individual sessions are always confidential. Thus Gertrude needed a good deal of individual work to overcome her fear that telling Terry would certainly destroy him. Some couples divorce to avoid confronting such a powerful emotional issue, while, paradoxically, others stay together for the same reason. If Gertrude had stayed with Terry, hiding her secret, their marriage would have been of the fragile bond variety—withdrawn and uncommunicative—one of the dysfunctional types of household described by Marilyn Little in *Family Breakup* (1982).

Since people daily make decisions by weighing the advantages against the disadvantages of each choice, one might hope that the decision to divorce could thus be made with some degree of mathematical accuracy. But unfortunately this is rarely the case. It may take a long time to sort out the well-hidden positives in an unhappy marriage, as well as less obvious resentments concealed beneath the initial complaints. Weighing the pros and cons is also difficult because many of the facts about divorcing are unknown. Costs, living arrangements, effects on children, and emotional consequences are all hard to predict. Part of our job is to help our clients become more clear about the outcome of either decision.

The first step in this process is to assess the positive potential in the marriage and the willingness of the two people to make changes in their *own* behavior. Usually they are all too ready to list the changes they want in their partners. Faced with a miserable, complaining couple or an angry, blaming pair a counselor may find it hard to see any positive signs in the welter of destructive interactions. Several ways to explore the resources are suggested by Virginia Satir in *Conjoint Family Therapy* (1983), a goldmine of recommendations for counselors. I use her method of asking each person how they happened to pick each other. Remembering these earlier feelings of attraction lets them focus on something other than grievances. Next I like to ask each person what they appreciate about the other and what each can do for the spouse that really pleases the other. Dissatisfied people may hesitate for a long time before answering these questions. The degree of embarrassment and the length of time before answering give clues to the positive commitment of the pair as well as to their ability to put their feelings into words. For example, a husband might say that what his wife likes best is for him to stay out of her way. Then I ask the wife to check this out and correct it if it is wrong. If it is hard for these discouraged people to remember what the partner likes best, or what they most appreciate in the other, then it has clearly been a long time since positive strokes were exchanged. And if their answers are completely off base, then I have a good hint as to how poorly they understand each other's wishes. Still the search for positives may relieve some of the tension so that the initial interview may proceed more smoothly.

As for the complaints, clients are ready to bring up the causes of friction that have led them to the brink of dissolution. These include financial problems, interfering parents, infidelity, alcoholism, abusive behavior, and personality traits such as vindictiveness, jealousy, and irresponsibility. Whether or not any of these liabilities will break up a marriage depends not so much on its severity as on one's *attitude* toward it, and on one's frustration tolerance. Alice, for example, called off her brief marriage after one drunken episode, viewing it as utterly inexcusable and the end of her husband's love. But no one has counted the number of people who will tolerate and care for an alcoholic spouse for many years, perhaps enjoying their own saintly patience. Similarly, Eric, an unassertive husband, left his wife after two years of being insulted and put down by his mother-in-law's weekly criticisms. Another husband might have joked with her and laughed at her insults, and still another might have simply confronted her with her behavior and asked her to stop it. Obviously each person gives a different meaning to the event. It is up to the counselor to find this emotional meaning and to see it through the client's eyes. Without this empathy it would be difficult to help couples understand each other.

Among the many disagreements that can begin the downward spiral of negative experiences, I sometimes find disappointed expectations of how a marriage *should* be, often based on the model of the parental marriages. Before Fred and Angela had gone too far in criticizing each other in their first interview I asked each one, "Is this the way it was in your family?" Their answers revealed that Fred was the product of a patriarchal family and saw himself as the breadwinner entitled to more privileges, more money, and more decision making than his wife. Angela came from a more democratic family and expected an equal share in the decisions. She saw her role as full-time homemaker and manager of social obligations as contributing just as much to the partnership as Fred's work. As a result she criticized Fred unmercifully and nagged him constantly about money. He scolded and both were so ready for divorce after only a year of marriage that they came into counseling with very little hope. I uncovered the fact that they married at nineteen, after a whirlwind courtship that included no discussion of plans for managing money or any other decisions. Each operated on the assumption that there was a right way (mine) and a wrong way (the other person's) and that the other should see the light and do things the right way. I pointed out that their parents had simply *chosen* to handle finances and other matters in their own ways, that there was no right way, and that Fred and Angela had chosen to follow their parents' methods. As Fred thought about his father's autocratic ways, he began to realize that he had really resented them. He saw that he was doing the same things that he disliked in his father and began to realize that he was trying to get his father's approval by following in his footsteps. As he changed, Angela, who had appeared more unyielding at first, was pleased and her nagging diminished. This helped Fred feel better about relinquishing some of his control and after several sessions the vicious circle of negative strokes moved in the opposite direction. Positive input led to more positive behavior in both partners.

If Fred and Angela's views of how a marriage should be had such high priority that neither would or could shift to a more accommodating attitude, then I would explore the emotional needs underlying their rigid stands. Angela, for example, might feel that she would give up her self-respect and identity if she acceded even an inch to Fred, and Fred might feel that he could not change without giving up his manhood and self-esteem. Then I would point out that neither could make the other one change. If neither partner wanted to work on making their own changes, I would let them know that counseling could not make the marriage rewarding. As they began to see that they could not fulfill each other's expectations, they might stop blaming each other and the counselor for not improving the relationship, and accept the fact that it takes two to make a marriage. They might even part with more sadness than rancor.

The case of Fred and Angela is a good example of the havoc that may follow when people see their wishes and wants as shoulds, oughts, and musts. I see many marital situations in which an important part of my job is to point out that shoulds are not laws—they are preferences and desires. Couples can argue endlessly about opinions or what should or should not be in a marriage, but there is no arguing about feelings or wishes. They are neither right nor wrong. I often ask couples to practice converting their shoulds into wishes. For example, instead of saying "He *should* treat me as an equal," Angela could learn to say "I would *like* to be an equal partner." This helps the couple to understand each other and removes a roadblock to negotiating as they find how much easier it is to accept the partner's wishes than the shoulds. I strongly recommend that "should-ridden" couples read *A New Guide to Rational Living* (Ellis and Harper 1977) for an attack on the power of the shoulds, oughts, and musts.

While Fred was able to give up his wish to follow his father's path, some clients have a need to control that is more tenacious and pervasive than the habit of following a family pattern. Fortunately some couples choose each other with complementary expectations of who will be in charge. A woman brought up in a patriarchal home may fit in gracefully with an authoritarian husband, enjoying the fact that he relieves her of the responsibility for decision making. Such a lopsided arrangement, however, may not stand up well over time. Eleanor, for example, had not finished college and had never held a job when she married Martin, ten years her senior. Martin took charge of all the family plans and Eleanor enjoyed his fatherly way of caring for her and the children. When the children reached adolescence and began to control their own activities, Eleanor decided to go back to school. Friction grew as the children defied their father's rule against rock music in the house, and Eleanor found new friends and activities outside the family. When she succeeded in finding a good job, she decided to give the children more freedom and more responsibilities. Martin no longer found himself the sole decision maker in the household and could not tolerate the changed situation.

While Eleanor's expectations of the marriage changed, Martin's did not. He came for one counseling session with Eleanor but rather than seek to change his role in the family he insisted that the others change. He found some comfort in talking it over with a sympathetic young woman in his office and soon decided to leave Eleanor for his co-worker who was as dependent as Eleanor had been twenty years earlier. Since Eleanor had been increasingly resentful of Martin and had entertained thoughts of divorce, it was not too difficult for her to accept Martin's decision to leave. Still, this could not be described as an amicable dissolution since both continued to resent the other's unwillingness to change. Like many people, Martin had not been able to learn that two people can cooperate comfortably as equals. To lose control over others caused him great anxiety. Such a person may need a long time in therapy to gain a sense of trust in other people, and to believe that he will not always be put down if he is not on top. This "top dog" versus "under dog" attitude is an example of the thinking that makes accommodation and sharing so difficult in many marriages.

Probably easier to deal with are the couples whose decision to divorce is based on poor communication. "We just can't communicate" has become a cliché. Actually it is impossible for two people in the same space *not* to communicate even though the message may be a wish to cut off communication. Communication is not a goal in itself. People may talk constantly yet feel cut off from each other. Usually what unhappy couples mean is that they do not share each other's wishes and feelings. If they cannot make their expectations, fears, hurts, and values clear to each other, how can they make a sensible decision about their shared life? If one is not sure what the partner wants, likes, or dislikes, how can one decide whether or not to live with that person?

Sometimes people fail to communicate because of their romantic notion that love makes it unnecessary. How often have counselors heard such complaints as, "If she really loved me, she would know that I want her to kiss me," or "If he loved me, he would know that I want him to help with the dishes." In fact, as every counselor has discovered, mind-reading is rampant among couples. But while many comfortable partners know each other's reactions before a word is spoken, the tendency of dysfunctional couples is to read each other wrong and to fail to check out their assumptions. On the way to helping a couple decide about divorce, counselors may have to give some basic training in communication. They can teach the couple to be clear and specific. Instead of generalizations such as "She shows me no consideration," the client might say, "She doesn't call me when she has to work late." Couples can be taught to listen without interrupting and to paraphrase in order to receive the message correctly. Instead of heaping criticism they can learn to ask for the changes they would like. To understand each other's feelings, husband and wife can reverse roles and express each other's complaints and criticisms—a difficult but very illuminating exercise for both. Another difficult task is learning to express feelings instead of opinions.

Some couples find anger particularly hard to express because they believe you never get angry at the one you love. In their book *Mirages of Marriage* Lederer and Jackson (1968) describe these and other mistaken assumptions that can cause great disappointments in marriage. Grace and Joe came close to divorce because of their misconception about anger but fortunately came into counseling before taking the step. As so often happens, the arrival of their first baby opened up new areas of conflict in their previously serene relationship. Grace, eager to prove herself a good mother, assumed that Joe did not want to be bothered with caring for his new son and that she had no right to ask him for help. She took complete charge, feeling noble about sparing him the feeding and diapering chores. But as her workload became heavier, she began to tell herself "If he really loved me, he would see that I'm tired out, and he would offer to help." Joe, on the other hand, really wanted more part in caring for the baby but saw Grace as insisting on doing it all and shutting him out. Assuming that in a loving marriage one does not rock the boat or start an argument, Joe said nothing and his resentment grew. Grace said nothing and her resentment grew too. Both felt thoroughly misunderstood, but instead of putting their feelings into words, they acted in increasingly irritating ways. Grace took to spending weekend time with women friends, taking the baby with her, while Joe began to work later than necessary at the office. Both rolled over and went to sleep every night without so much as a goodnight kiss. Thoughts of divorce entered their heads.

My job was to first help them see that negative feelings are inevitable in any close relationship and to encourage them to express their wants directly. Very cautiously they began to tell each other exactly how they felt about the baby care situation. They also began to learn a new attitude toward anger. Both had believed the old myth that one never gets angry at a loved one. Both had held back, fearful of displeasing the other. To their surprise, being open about their feelings did not have the disastrous results they dreaded, but led to a real increase in their understanding of each other. They were also surprised to learn that they had actually been expressing anger through their passive, distancing behavior. Sharing resentments soon allowed positive feelings to return and the divorce each had contemplated was forgotten. They even did a little mild exploding at each other at home, prompting Grace's remark "I found that getting mad at my husband wasn't the end of the world."

More difficult than helping quiet people like Grace and Joe to be more expressive is working with a couple on the decision to divorce when both are open in pouring out their anger at each other. David and Deanna, in their thirties, were pleasant, attractive people when seen separately, but fought so loudly in joint sessions that nearby office workers complained of the noise. Counterattacks followed each angry criticism, and neither stopped long enough to listen to the other. These shouting matches plus episodes of pushing and shoving had been going on for ten years. Why would such a hostile couple stay together for so many years? Sorting out some of their complaints, I asked Deanna "What is the worst thing that could happen if Dave works on Saturday instead of being with you and the children" and I asked David "What is the worst that could happen if Deanna goes into the bedroom and slams the door?" Exploration of their fantasies revealed that both of these needful people felt extremely anxious when there was the slightest hint that they might be alone and abandoned. Both had felt rejected by angry, explosive parents, but neither had been aware of their intense fear of abandonment, only of the anger it triggered. Their fights served a purpose—arguing kept them intimately involved. They chose not to explore their anxious feelings, which would have meant hard therapeutic work. Instead, they continued in their volatile marriage, separating several times but always returning. I had expected them to divorce and with some difficulty I had to accept that this was the kind of marriage they chose.

If angry couples can learn to express their negative feelings without insulting each other, they are making progress toward understanding each other and making a healthier marriage. If a client can learn to say "I get lonely when you go off every Saturday—I really get burned up!" instead of "You're always thinking of yourself—go ahead, but don't be surprised if I'm not here when you get back!" this gives the counselor a clue to the viability of the marriage, as it reveals the clients' willingness to share vulnerable feelings and to give up retaliating.

As important as communicating about negative feelings in a close relationship is expressing one's expectations about love and sexuality. Differences and misunderstandings in this area can lead a couple in the direction of divorce. The sexual revolution of the 1960s, with the new openness about sexual matters, has apparently left many couples unaffected. If a pair is considering divorce and their complaints do not include sexual problems, it is important for the counselor to ask about this aspect of their lives, which can hardly be unaffected by their emotional difficulties. The counselor's willingness to speak openly and objectively about sex will encourage clients to discuss their feelings. Using Rogerian methods of listening and paraphrasing will elicit their differing expectations in this area. The old cliché "Women give sex in exchange for love, and men give love in exchange for sex" may not fit all cases, but in my experience women place a higher value than men on loving words and on hugging and cuddling for its own sake rather than as a prelude to intercourse. Some husbands feel awkward at putting their love into words. When one wife asked her reticent husband "Do you really love me" he responded impatiently "I'm here, aren't I." He did love her but she was not reassured. For some men, having sex with their wives is a clear way of expressing their love so they find preliminary words unnecessary. More than one woman client has told me that she wants to hug and kiss her husband more often, but refrains "Because if I do, he always takes it as a signal, and wants to go straight to bed." Another complaint I've heard from women is "After we've quarreled, he thinks that all he has to do to make up and show he's sorry is to have sex." To such a woman, sex after a quarrel without any appropriate discussion is not only insufficient but repugnant. Paradoxically, while craving words from her partner she may punish him with the silent treatment. Nearly a century since Freud has opened the door to the acceptance of sexuality as an important reality and more than twenty years since sex has become a household word, some couples still cannot reveal their sexual wishes until the safety of the counselor's office gives them permission.

Before a couple can decide whether these issues will break up their marriage they may need help to get rid of some old myths and misconceptions such as "Women aren't supposed to take the initiative," and "Real men aren't romantic." A good deal of questioning of these assumptions may be needed before the couple can be open with each other about sexual wishes.

Couples whose main complaint is sexual problems are probably having interpersonal troubles as well. Ned and Wanda, an assertive twenty-year-old pair, quarreled because Ned wanted sex much more often than Wanda, and at times inconvenient for her. As I explored the ways in which they had tried to solve the problem, it became clear that neither Ned nor Wanda was willing to compromise. This rigid, ungiving attitude permeated their other interactions. Had this been a matter mainly of sexual timing, it might have been solvable, but it was actually a symptom of a more basic lack in the marriage.

Both Ned and Wanda were more committed to seeking their own pleasure than to making a good relationship. With this couple I used the concept of the three ego states described by Eric Berne in *Transactional Analysis in Psychotherapy* (1961). We all have a Parent ego state that can be critical or nurturing, and a Child ego state that may be fearful and dependent or spontaneous and playful. Our Adult ego state processes information and solves problems in a reasonable, business-like way. In *Born to Win* (1971) James and Jongeward give a very useful explanation of this system. I made Ned and Wanda aware that they were blaming each other in a critical Parent manner and demanding their own way as negative Children instead of working on the conflict with their rational, problem-solving, Adult ego states. In counseling, the task is often to find and support the Adult part as it struggles to take charge. But with Ned and Wanda, each was quick to accuse the other of operating as a Child and unwilling to work on developing a more objective Adult stance. And since marriage is for adults, Ned and Wanda soon separated, each blaming the other for the unsatisfactory relationship. Couples who understand and accept each other's sexual attitudes, and want to continue in a marriage that is satisfactory except for sexual problems are in a very different situation, and for them I recommend referral to a qualified sex therapist for study of the sexual difficulty.

One of the most threatening problems related to sex is the discovery of infidelity, a crisis that often brings a couple in for help on the decision to divorce. Counselors may have strong opinions about extramarital affairs, based on religious views, moral values, or their own emotional reactions. It may help counselors to be more open and less judgmental to realize that infidelity is not one monolithic concept. It can mean a one-time fling at an out-of-town convention (jokingly referred to as conventional behavior), an occasional episode with a friend, a long-standing liaison complete with a separate apartment and list of alibis, or it may mean a deep and satisfying relationship far more important than the marriage. It is hardly realistic to hold the same attitude toward each of these widely differing situations.

In any event, the first step is to explore the meaning of the infidelity to each partner, which may require separate interviews for clients so fearful of the other's reaction that they hesitate to reveal all the facts. If the extramarital behavior carried the same meaning for both partners, the problem might not be serious. Couples who can accept a completely open marriage will not seek help; likewise a religious couple, both strongly opposed to infidelity, might weather the upset and be able to reconcile with or without professional help if the strayed one is really repentant and the other partner is truly forgiving. I worked with one couple who agreed to accept sexual encounters outside of their marriage since both believed that areas of independence were important. The agreement and the marriage both broke down, however, when the wife fell in love and wished to continue a serious relationship with another man.

In my work with couples close to divorce I have seen them attach many different meanings to infidelity. One person may feel that an affair actually contributes to the marriage by providing necessary variety or by making an unexciting marriage more tolerable. Another may see the affair as having no effect on his or her continuing love for the spouse, much like a diverting hobby. Others may see outside affairs as a necessary way of having more frequent sexual outlets. Some see any infidelity as a totally unjustified intrusion into marriage territory and as a failure to honor the marriage commitment. These people may react with feelings of inadequacy, as though the partner's behavior were a direct slap at their attractiveness, and expressions of anger and outrage are likely. Still others, although shocked and feeling cast aside, may be willing to explore the causes of the unfaithfulness and try to understand their partner's position.

On the other hand, some people claim that they can successfully hide infidelities from their spouses, believing that "What you don't know won't hurt you." Perhaps this is true for some, but I think it is much more likely that when one is hiding an important aspect of oneself from a marriage partner, there will be some loss of intimacy and increase in emotional distance. The partner is bound to feel the change unless the relationship is already quite devoid of intimacy. If the unfaithful one feels guilty, he or she may somehow let the spouse "accidentally" find out. To some, the lying that is usually necessary to hide an affair is more damaging than the sexual infidelity. Dishonesty may be intolerable to the faithful partner and may cause intolerable guilt in the other.

To defuse the turbulent emotions surrounding the crisis I ask the couple to look at some facts such as the difference between feelings and actions. Without condoning the actions, I point out that anyone can easily be attracted to more than one member of the opposite sex and that it is not sinful for sexual feelings to be aroused. It is not surprising that husbands are more often involved than wives since men usually have more opportunities outside the home and traditionally take the initiative in sexual encounters. It can be helpful to suggest to a homemaker wife that if the situation were reversed and she had an efficient, good-looking young man in the house helping her with chores and children from nine to five, the chances of her having an affair might increase to the level of the traditional liaisons between businessmen and their secretaries, or physicians and their nurses.

While feelings of attraction can be harmless, acting on these temptations has damaged or destroyed many marriages. Exploring why a person feels impelled to act on the sexual impulses uncovers a variety of reasons such as disappointment in the partner, sexual frustration, feeling overcontrolled, or a need to be seen as attractive to more than one person. One often hears condoning comments such as "She couldn't have been a good wife or he wouldn't have needed an affair," which can lead to unnecessary self-blame on the part of the "wronged" partner. In our still sexist society we are less likely to hear the husband blamed for the wife's infidelity. In either case I remind the clients that no one can be responsible for another adult's actions. The one who took action had a clear choice to control or not to control the behavior. In my opinion, there are no uncontrollable urges except in very young children or the mentally incompetent. Even if a wife were hostile and withdrawn and her husband felt miserable and emotionally deprived, he had other options to solve the problem. He could try to understand the reasons for his wife's hostility or if communication failed he could seek counseling. If his wife refused to consider help, he could go for help by himself. Another option would be to tell his wife clearly that the situation was intolerable for him and unless there were changes he would have to leave. Having an affair was not his only option.

When an affair brings a couple to the verge of divorce, the crisis may be an opportunity to open lines of communication and to share dissatisfactions so that the couple may do some valuable reconstructive work on the relationship. Hiding their complaints, they give each other no chance to improve. A case in point is that of Hilda and Arthur. Arthur was expecting some important letters when he was away on a business trip. He telephoned home and asked Hilda to open his mail and read it to him, not anticipating that a glowing love letter from another woman would be forwarded from his office to his home. Hilda, thoroughly committed to their marriage of twelve years with two children, was horrified. Arthur was upset and confused. Hilda thought seriously of divorce but neither she nor Arthur wanted to end the marriage so they came for counseling. Arthur had married Hilda when she was young and shy, and had enjoyed being her mentor and protector. After marrying, Hilda, a youngest child who always felt left out of family decisions, found herself in charge of things for the first time in her life. She thoroughly enjoyed being the household boss, and went from decision maker in matters of food and floor wax to choosing which movies the couple would see and which house to buy. Arthur felt pushed out of his former dominant position but saw himself as a nice guy, and even after the arrival of children worsened the situation, he did not complain. Instead, he had an affair. Was the affair Hilda's fault for being so controlling or Arthur's for not telling her his objections? Why should Hilda change if Arthur did not object?

In counseling both Arthur and Hilda realized that Arthur had become more and more withdrawn. Gradually I helped Arthur learn that he could express his dislike of Hilda's behavior without creating the catastrophe he feared, which was in fact less destructive than the havoc caused by the affair. Slowly, he began to see that the good guy image cut him off from experiencing an important part of himself—his negative feelings—and interfered with the real intimacy he longed for in the marriage.

Hilda was badly shaken but was willing to look at her own behavior. To explore her exaggerated need to be in charge I asked her to focus on the feeling she would have if others had to be in control and to describe the image that came to mind. Tears came to her eyes as she described the picture that occurred to her. She saw herself as a little girl arguing with her mother about a dress she did not like. Her mother had bought the dress despite Hilda's pleading and made her wear it. Hilda remembered how intensely she wanted to choose a different dress and how devalued and powerless she felt, not only then but on other occasions when she was left out of decisions. Counseling helped Hilda see that she was no longer the helpless child who needed to prove her worth by taking charge of everything. She also saw, much to her disgust, that she had been taking on her dominating mother's Critical Parent role in the way she ran her household. I used the transactional analysis framework to help her see herself as the competent adult woman she was who did not need to feel threatened by sharing decisions with Arthur.

As this couple worked in counseling the affair lost its central importance and became more a symptom of their real problems than a reason for divorce. While painful, the crisis gave Hilda and Arthur an opportunity to reassess and understand themselves, and to take steps toward working out a more comfortable marriage. Although these two enjoyed a happy ending, other cases of infidelity may be a by-product of a relationship that no longer provides any emotional supplies. If a person is already receiving a great amount of gratification from the new lover there is little incentive to do the hard work of self assessment and a divorce may be inevitable. The other marriage partner may be willing to explore the problems and to make changes but this is not enough. One person alone cannot make a good marriage yet it takes only one to bring about a divorce.

Less dramatic than discovering infidelity as a prelude to the end of a marriage are the slow changes in a couple that gradually erode the relationship. Since everyone's attitudes and habits change over time, it must be that in marriages making it to the fiftieth anniversary the growth and changes in each partner have been compatible. But couples who come for divorce counseling have often changed in ways that seem irreconcilable. Beth and Dean illustrate a common pattern. Inseparable in high school, they danced, studied, and went to football games together. After graduation Beth started college and Dean went in the service. When he returned they married right away, deciding that Dean would go to college using his GI benefits while Beth would drop out and go to work, then finish her education later. After Dean got his degree and found a good job they started a family. They were happy for many years together, working on their house and yard, spending evenings together, and taking the three children on weekend outings. Then Dean was promoted and transferred to a large city where his colleagues introduced him to a more sophisticated way of life. Soon he met local politicians and decided to run for a county office. Beth, who had been busy with her house and children, had long since shelved her college plans. She found she did not like the city, did not understand the cocktail party conversation, and did not dress as stylishly as the other corporate wives who expected her to support the opera, which she did not enjoy. She complained to Dean about going to company parties and complained when he went without her. She resented his out-of-town business trips and his weekend meetings with political committees. He began to be ashamed of his stay-at-home wife, and found himself taking longer business trips than was necessary.

When their conflict brought them into counseling, Beth's complaint was that Dean did not give enough time to the family. Dean complained that Beth did not understand his obligations and did not support him by learning to enjoy his new friends and his new activities. Each felt pressured, unloved, and abandoned. In such a case I had to assess their openness to change and their willingness to accept their differences if no changes were made. First, I helped Beth and Dean sort out the difference between the realities in the situation and their own unrealistic expectations of each other. It was a fact that Dean enjoyed his work and his new interest in politics, and would feel resentful and unfulfilled if he had to give up either. It was also a fact that Beth wanted to enjoy more family time with Dean and that she saw family activities as more important than Dean's new interests. Another fact for both to face was Beth's dislike of Dean's new social life. As for their expectations of each other, Dean wanted a wife who shared his enthusiasms and Beth wanted a husband who loved to spend his free time with the family. As we explored their feelings, Beth described how hypocritical and uncomfortable she felt at the business and social events so important to Dean, and he admitted that he was restless and uncommunicative when he gave up some of his activities to be with Beth and the children.

After several sessions Dean was able to explain that he wanted to spend more time with the family but Beth's criticisms and lack of support turned him away. Her refusal to take an interest in his career had finally reduced his love and respect for her to the vanishing point. With tears in her eyes Beth then said that she wanted to be supportive of Dean but he had changed since the transfer. She no longer felt the warmth and admiration she had for him before he became so aggressively ambitious. She saw him as trying to turn her into a corporate wife instead of appreciating her for herself. Counseling helped them to see that they had pressured and pushed each other away. The next step was to help them see that their attempts to change each other by criticism and coercion were both futile and alienating. One can only change oneself. It was difficult for them to accept this fact and to realize that the other partner was not going to change. Dean was not willing to give up his new role—he felt that he could not be himself if he had to. Beth, too, knew that she could not be the person she wanted to be if she conformed to Dean's wishes. This confrontation was sad but I pointed out that both would be kind to allow each other to retain their dignity as persons and to give each other the opportunity to find more congenial partners. As their counseling sessions gradually helped them see that they could not fulfill each other's wishes, both were able to accept dissolution, although painful, as more satisfactory than marriage. After the separation, Dean found new enjoyment in being with his children since they were no longer part of the tense home atmosphere that had kept him aloof. The crisis forced Beth to reassess herself and she decided to go back to school to get training for a satisfying career. Follow-up a few months later found Beth not only enjoying her classes, but making new friends.

Another kind of change I have seen in marriages happens when the traits endearing the couple to each other in courtship days become less lovable and even repugnant in the long haul of shared living space. A good example is the marriage of Richard and Jana, both twenty-eight. A nasty argument over whether or not to have a baby brought them to counseling. Richard was a serious, reticent, young professor whose strength and dependability had appealed to Jana. She felt a sense of security with him that she had lacked in her own disorganized family. To Richard, Jana's charming spontaneity and fun-loving nature gave him a welcome change from his academic pursuits and she led the way in a courtship of dancing, skiing, and parties. Five years later in counseling Jana complained that Richard was always studying, never talked to her, and hardly ever wanted to go out. Richard no longer found Jana's spontaneity charming as checks bounced because she forgot to balance the checkbook. She invited people over for the evening on the spur of the moment when Richard wanted to read and her chatter interrupted him when he was studying. Those traits that had seemed so attractive before did not wear well around the house. People like this pair, without realizing it, have found mates who make up for their own deficiencies. Jana was short on ability to put brakes on her impulses and to structure her life; Richard was rigid in his habits and inhibited in expressing himself. At one point I could not help saying "If I could put the two of you together, you might make a well-rounded person!"

This remark hit home with both of them. Jana began to see that she expected Richard to provide the limits and stability she would not provide for herself. Richard became aware that he needed to unbend and allow himself to be more relaxed, and that Jana could not do this for him. Both were amazed to find that they were criticizing each other for doing the jobs they had assigned to each other in the first place. Since both were willing to work on their respective deficiencies, once these were pointed out, they were able to become more understanding and tolerant. Positive exchanges began to return to the marriage and divorce plans were dropped.

A similar marriage that produced a different outcome was that of Katherine, another blithe spirit whose casual attitude fascinated Wayne, her proper husband. Before they married in their early twenties, Katherine joked that Wayne would be good for her, that he would teach her good manners. Sharing a home was disillusioning for both. Wayne found that Katherine's casualness included a laissez faire approach to cooking and housekeeping. He could not tolerate her scattering of clothes, cosmetics, and the incoming mail about the house; she could not put up with his insistence on neatness and a scheduled life. They had been married less than two years when the resentments and recriminations escalated into threats of divorce. When they came for counseling I saw that, like Richard and Jana, each had looked to the other for traits they lacked, and each had gotten more than they bargained for. I helped them look at their one-sidedness and we explored their willingness to change. After several sessions, Katherine said that she would feel she was in a straitjacket if she had to give up her easygoing ways. Wayne wanted no part of being sloppy and saw no need to relax his standards. Orderliness and neatness were an important part of his self-image. Neither Katherine nor Wayne could see a solution unless the other one changed and they proceeded to obtain a dissolution. Both of these couples cared for each other. The main difference I saw was that Katherine and Wayne felt too threatened by change whereas Richard and Jana, more secure in their self-acceptance, were not as fearful of being hurt by making changes.

Sometimes the real problems in a marriage are hidden by the surface conflicts that a couple brings in as their presenting complaints. Money is often cited as a cause of marital disruption, meaning usually that for each person money has an entirely different significance. William and Jessie came for counseling because Jessie threatened to leave if William refused to put his savings in a joint bank account. Both were in their thirties, had been married before, and were making good salaries. In their first sessions they poured out a confusing mass of facts and figures about their earnings, their expenses, how much William had saved, and how much Jessie was willing to put into the joint account. I could not understand much less answer their questions on what was fair in their financial matters, so angry and vituperative were their exchanges, but persistent questioning eventually revealed the real issues. It turned out that Jessie was not concerned with the amount of money since she knew she could support herself and save for her future; to her, William's money was a symbol of his commitment. If he would not share his savings then she believed he was not really committed to the marriage. William insisted that he loved Jessie and wanted to keep the marriage, but he explained that he had grown up in a very poor family, had made a good deal of money in the business he owned, and had lost most of it in his previous divorce. To him, money meant security. Even more important, he finally revealed that he would not put his savings in a joint account because he feared that Jessie could then take it all away from him. He simply did not trust her. Thus William's real issues stemmed from his life-long lack of security and fear of trusting people. No matter that Jessie loved him, she could never meet these needs of his. Her issues were similar—she could not feel secure in the relationship unless she had proof of her husband's commitment. To her this proof had to be tangible. When I helped them clarify the real meaning of money in the bank, they decided, but not amicably, that dissolution was their best choice. Their marriage lacked an essential element for survival of a marriage—trust. And neither felt secure enough to face the difficult task of self-appraisal and change.

Next to money and sex, children often pose the biggest threat to a marriage. It is not surprising that there is a peak in divorces after the birth of the first child when roles suddenly change, expenses increase, and the house seems to be full of more work and less space. Because of the unrealistic expectation that parenting will be *all* pride and joy, new parents may be reluctant to admit that babies are not always as adorable as advertised. Counseling such new parents involves exploring the meaning of the new roles to each partner. A mother may see herself as pushed into a demeaning slave role or a young father may feel discarded in favor of the newcomer. As a result, both may feel guilty and depressed.

An important job for the counselor is to help the couple accept these negative feelings as natural if not inevitable in the midst of the disruptions, hard work, and lack of sleep a baby can cause. After one new mother tearfully described her disappointment and irritation with her colicky, crying baby, I responded with "I'll bet there are times when you would just like to throw him out the window!" Her jaw dropped in disbelief. I could almost hear her thinking, "How could a *therapist* say such a thing!" Then she began to smile and she relaxed with a big sigh. I had given her permission to own her angry feelings toward her infant, and she became more accepting of herself, the baby, and her husband, toward whom her crabbiness had spread. I used this technique successfully with other parents whose annoyance with their babies and older children as well had threatened to ruin their marriages. In other cases the arrival of children brings up unresolved issues with the couple's own parents, with whom they now suddenly may find themselves identifying. Young parents may need to become aware of their own unsatisfied needs for love before they can freely love their children. The additional difficulties of raising a handicapped or developmentally disabled child can cause so much disappointment, guilt, and resentment in parents that their marriage may be disrupted to the point of divorce.

For new parents I recommend group counseling where they can find support and practical advice from other mothers and fathers who are struggling with the tremendous changes a first child brings. Religious differences that may have been resolved before the arrival of children force a couple to again review this matter. If each partner feels strongly about a religion it may not be possible to compromise by exposing the children to both religions and letting them choose as they get older. If divorce follows a bitter custody battle may take place since the custodial parent will be able to choose the child's religious experiences. If the couple wishes to forestall such an outcome, the counselor's job is to explore whether the issue is purely one of strongly held religious values or whether the common need to control is motivating the parents. Uncovering the irrational beliefs that create the need to be in control may diminish the "top dog" attitude and help the couple learn to cooperate as equals and to find a solution acceptable to both.

Conversely, another crisis may occur when the last child leaves home and the couple, whose conflicts may have been buffered for years by the presence of their children, find themselves face to face with each other and their differences. George and Anna were in their sixties before their thoughts of divorce came out in the open and they came into counseling for the first time. George's work had taken him away from home on frequent trips and when he was home family recreation had favored camping, picnics, and other activities the children enjoyed. This left little time for George and Anna to do things by themselves. Since the children lived at home while going to college and getting started in their careers, George was nearing retirement before the youngest of their four daughters left home. At last he was ready to take Anna on some interesting trips and try out some new hobbies. He took tennis lessons and joined a book club. Anna, on the other hand, would not accept the empty nest, and went every day to help their married daughters who lived in the same city. She cared for her grandchildren, took her daughters shopping, and sewed for the family. She claimed that she could not go on trips because she was needed at home, and told George that she did not have time for the book club and had no interest in tennis. George had looked forward to a carefree retirement but Anna would not give up her mothering role to be a companion. Their wishes were so antithetical that they could not find a satisfactory middle way. In counseling I helped them see and accept the unfortunate fact that they were no longer as important to each other as they had been in the past, and that each could carve out satisfying separate lifestyles. They did a good deal of blaming and trying to persuade each other before they reluctantly gave up the struggle and decided to separate.

Some therapists have developed well structured exercises to help a couple decide whether or not to divorce. Marjorie Kawin Toomin prescribes a three month separation with counseling for these couples. She sees distance and space as an opportunity to explore themselves and the relationship. During this period she asks the couple not to see a lawyer and to make no permanent decisions. They are to see each other when both wish to and are to explore relationships with other men and women. She claims that couples become more honest and open with each other and they also discover that separation or divorce might not be as catastrophic as they had imagined. Toomin has found that viable relationships not only survive this structured separation, but couples often find a new, more satisfying way of being together. To understand this method I recommend that counselors study Toomin's article entitled "Separation Counseling" in *Creative Divorce through Social and Psychological Approaches* by Hardy and Cull (1974).

Dr. Gordon Harshman, a psychologist writing in Cull and Hardy's 1974 book, *Deciding on Divorce,* suggests a time-consuming set of exercises to improve self-understanding and decision making. The couple is to list the activities they like, together and separately, and to list what they will gain and lose by staying together. After comparing lists they go on to self-understanding exercises—keeping a log of their feelings and reactions, jotting down their own assets and weaknesses, goals and values. Next they are to list what they like and resent about each other. Harshman details several other exercises and instructs the couple to discuss the results after each step.

Another therapist pair, Norman and Betty Byfield Paul of Boston, use creative separation of four months to help couples think through the decision to divorce. One value of the method is that people discover what it would mean to support two households. While separated, they work in therapy on problems stemming from their relationships with their own parents. Dr. and Mrs. Paul, quoted in the *Marriage and Divorce Today Newsletter* (May 17, 1982, p. 1), emphasize the need to end the "continual quest for new partners who are expected to provide the nourishing that the father or mother did not." Of forty couples who used creative separation, twenty-eight marriages changed for the better and the other twelve achieved an amicable dissolution.

After a couple has finally decided to end their marriage there will be less stress if each party can sort out, verbalize, and accept what happened in the marriage so that the past can be laid to rest. The counselor can help the individuals to remember that the choice of a partner was in many ways a good one at the time—no one would marry a person without any redeeming features at all! The couple freely chose each other and were in love at the time. The counselor can point out that both were in an earlier stage of their lives at that time and that living together revealed traits that neither may have been aware of before. Both developed in new directions so that positive and negative interactions alternated over the years. They did not always like the other's new choices but no one can control another person's preferences and values.

An important job for the counselor is to work on diluting blame and combatting the idea that either person is at fault for having different expectations of the marriage or for having different wishes, values, and family programming. No one is to blame for having been taught to hide feelings or to express negative emotions in destructive ways. And if a partner did not choose to change, very likely he or she had a real reason for being afraid to take that difficult step. Realizing this, the other member of the pair may be able to feel more regret than blame.

The mixture of positive and negative feelings makes ending any relationship difficult, but after the dissolution each is free to make new choices as to the kind of person each wants to be. And if the counseling has been helpful, the client has probably grown in some new directions already and is beginning, at least tentatively, to venture into forming a new life.

3
The One-Sided Decision

Often a client chooses to come in alone to sort out confused feelings about a marriage. He or she may want to look at the pros and cons without the spouse present to inject another opinion. Or the spouse may have refused to come in, claiming that the partner is at fault. In that case, I usually ask the spouse to come in, and have had some success by pointing out that I need the other point of view and that it will be helpful in working on the wife's or husband's problems. I try to do this at the beginning of treatment before a strong bond has developed between the client and myself. Otherwise the person who is not in treatment may see me as allied with his or her partner, which will make joint counseling more difficult.

While I naturally empathize with a client who describes a very unhappy situation, it is important to remember that there is another side to the story. I learned this in an extreme way through evaluating couples in custody conflicts. If the first person I see describes the dreadful insults she has suffered at the hands of her totally insensitive husband, I tend to sympathize with her. When the husband comes in, I am prepared for an interview with a psychopath. To my surprise he may turn out to be a meek, unassertive man who has put up with his wife's neglect and infidelities for years. It is hard to believe that these two are talking about the same marriage. But both may be right. It is easy to overlook or minimize one's own faults.

Many of the people who come in alone have hesitated for years to do anything about an unsatisfactory marriage because they may minimize their partner's faults and blame themselves for the unhappy relationship. Some have waited a long time before coming into counseling and some continue to hesitate even after counseling clarifies the issues. Doris, for example, discussed and weighed the idea of divorce for more than two years in counseling. She was unhappy with John, her very uncommunicative and withdrawn husband, but she respected his ability as a prominent scientist and a reasonably good father to their two small children. Three times during counseling she gathered up her courage and went to a lawyer. The first time, the lawyer prepared the necessary papers to start the proceedings. This jolted John into showing some affection and willingness to share so she called off the dissolution. After a few months the relationship deteriorated again and Doris went back to her lawyer. The same papers were there, ready to be signed. Again John changed his ways but not for long. After a third visit to the lawyers, followed by the same temporary improvement, Doris, who had continued in counseling, was able to tell John that if he did not do some serious changing, she would definitely separate. This finally brought John into counseling. A few sessions helped him reduce his fear of opening up and his fear of rejection if he became intimate. Soon after this counseling the couple moved to an area they both liked. When I heard from Doris some months later there was no mention of divorce. Three years later she telephoned, again wavering, wanting a dissolution but unable to take the step. I have known other clients who, faced with legal papers, suddenly backed down from their decision. The truth of the legal finality was too hard to face. Doris, after some months of counseling with another therapist, returned to the Seattle area and announced that she had divorced John. Relieved of her vacillation and indecisiveness, she was enthusiastically reorganizing her life and felt no further need for counseling.

In working with a client alone, I listen to the litany of grievances, then ask what the person has done to communicate these feelings to the partner and to make requests for changes. Often the clients believe they have done everything possible to improve the marriage, but this may consist of simply nagging the partner for years, rather than making constructive changes. Usually the client is so ambivalent about the relationship that I need to help sort out the pros and cons of the situation. Clients may not be in touch with their own important wishes and deeply held values. To clarify these, I ask clients to list the priorities they demand or wish for in a relationship and to note which ones are fulfilled and which are not. It is surprising to find that sometimes people are not even aware of their priorities. Pat, for example, had been married for fifteen years and was nearing forty before she became increasingly dissatisfied with her marriage and turned to counseling. She explained that her husband, Charles, was constantly preoccupied with the business he owned and often gruff with her and their two boys. When Pat drew up her wish list for a good marriage she included being considerate, having a sense of humor, sharing chores, giving affection, being good with children, and enjoying recreation together. I suggested to Pat that some other qualities may be important such as a good sexual relationship, shared religion, physical attractiveness, and financial security. She added some of these to her list then rearranged the items with the most valued at the top and those more easily dispensed with at the bottom. Next I asked her to make a list of the things she actually had in her marriage. This second list forced her to see that affection, companionship, and good sex—top priorities on her list of wishes—were almost completely missing. "And I thought our marriage was as least seventy-five percent good" she commented in amazement. This exercise, of course, will not solve the undecided person's dilemma but it can serve to make the discrepancy between the real and the wished for marriage more striking. Pat had come a step closer to choosing a divorce but needed more time to resolve her ambivalence.

Next, we used the two-chair technique, described by Fritz Perls in *Gestalt Therapy Verbatim* (1969), to clarify the pros and cons of Pat's relationship with Charles. The two chairs faced each other and Pat sat first in the pro-marriage chair, telling the con part of herself that she should wait for the children to grow up, that she could not earn enough to live on her own, and that she really liked having Charles as an escort for concerts and parties. When she switched to the other chair her voice became more anguished—"But I don't really like him. He's cheated and lied, and he doesn't really pay any attention to the children when they need him." Back in the first chair she countered with "I know, but I like the house. I couldn't give it up and I couldn't live in it without his income. Besides, my parents like him, and he is terribly intelligent." She changed chairs again and in the unhappy tone argued "Intelligence doesn't help! And I'd be crazy to stay just for the sake of the house! I just don't get any real affection any more, and I don't enjoy sex with him—in fact I hate it!" After a few more of these arguments with herself, which became more and more emotional, it became clear to me and finally to Pat that most of Pat's positive feelings for Charles were gone, and that she was receiving no positive strokes and no emotional support from him.

Since she was still reluctant to make the break, we next explored what Pat could do herself to put back some positive feelings into the relationship. One cannot force feelings to change and no one can make another person alter basic personality traits, but living together is a reciprocal arrangement and Pat's behavior naturally had an effect on Charles. She examined her ways of relating to him and decided that she could be more cordial to him. She could explain what she wanted courteously rather than nagging and complaining as she had in the past. She gave up sulking silently, avoided retaliating when she felt mistreated, and stopped mediating between the boys and their father, letting that relationship find its own level. This approach paid off. Life became calmer at home and Pat picked up some of her own interests that she had dropped during the time of turmoil. In counseling she rehearsed describing her true feelings for Charles, or rather her lack of feelings for him. When he still refused to take part in counseling, it became clear to Pat that he was not going to contribute any more to the marriage than he had in the past. Soon Pat was able to end the marriage without the catastrophic uproar that she had anticipated. Although Pat's changed behavior could not modify Charles's self-centered personality, since he apparently wished to remain as he was, it did make their interactions smoother and their dissolution less destructive. Pat felt more at ease with herself and more competent to cope with life on her own since she had put a good deal of effort into understanding herself.

When I first suggested to Pat that changes on her part could be beneficial,

I heard the response often given by dissatisfied spouses—"Why should *I* have to do all the work? Why shouldn't *he*?" But when Pat began to moderate her communications with Charles, the improvement provided positive reinforcement for Pat to continue. Thus counselors can reassure such clients that this "work" will be for their own benefit.

Had Pat's dependency needs been stronger, the outcome might have been different. Recent studies of battered women enmeshed in marriages far more destructive than Pat's have revealed why some wives stay on for years, somehow tolerating an intolerable situation—or rather a situation that many counselors regard as intolerable. Often, although bruised and bloody, women blame themselves for the battering and strive to be better wives hoping that this will change their husbands. (After all, many of the saints were martyred before they were canonized.) Both men and women have suffered mental torture just as painful as physical beatings, or more so, and have coped with it for years. They are similar to abused children, who, after placement in a good foster home, run back to the parents who mistreated them. What are the pay-offs in living as a victim of abuse?

Sue Walen, a psychologist who has worked with dozens of people in unhappy marriages, has collected thirty-five reasons why such people, mainly women, do not seek a dissolution. These range from vague fears that divorce would be a big mistake to more concrete but often unrealistic fears that "He would take the children away and I'd never see them again," or "He would surely kill me if I left." In a 1981 lecture she described many of these reasons. Some clients avoid divorcing for fear of hurting the children, hurting their parents, or even hurting the insecure but reprehensible spouse. Other fears have to do with financial insecurity, loneliness, or inability to find a new mate. Some see divorce as a personal failure, destroying their self-esteem so that they cannot face friends and relatives. Some people have strong moral or religious injunctions against divorce, take "for better or worse" literally, and believe that they should work on the marriage no matter what. One unhappy woman stuck in a miserable situation said stoically "I've put up with it for fifteen years. I ought to be able to do it for fifteen more."

Dr. Walen also found a few vindictive people who persisted in the marriage because "I don't want to give him the satisfaction," or to prevent the other one from remarrying, or in the hope that the other would bear the onus of making the break. Some try to hurry divorce along by provoking the spouse into such exasperation that he or she will take the final step. While most of Dr. Walen's cases involved women, Morton Hunt, who has studied and written extensively about formerly married people, found that men also have a variety of reasons for avoiding dissolution. Men may console themselves with "That's life," or "Nothing's perfect" when a marriage is unrewarding. And men may more easily look the other way since they usually have more outside sources of satisfaction available—careers, sports, affairs—that take them away from the unhappy home.

Although many of the reasons for staying married are realistic, others are excuses that hide the real issues. Thus the counselor's job is to gather enough data to help clients become aware of the true reasons for staying in their cheerless circumstances. The fact that these people have sought help shows that they have not entirely convinced themselves that staying in the marriage is right. And it shows that they want relief from the uncomfortable ambivalence that is affecting their health, work, and dispositions.

As for the practical reasons that deter some clients, it is true that divorce is expensive and that two apart cannot live as cheaply as two together. In my experience, however, it is rarely the financial problems that tip the scales for or against dissolution. Thousands of determined women have survived and raised children on the income from unskilled jobs, Aid to Families with Dependent Children benefits, meager support payments, or a combination of these. Men determined to leave a marriage have found economical ways of living such as sharing a home with friends. I encourage my clients to explore the financial realities—the cost of lawyers, the housing situation, the cost of moving, the probable amount of child support, the job market, the cost of going back to school to learn new skills. Until a realistic budget is made it is not clear whether financial problems are the real obstacle or whether fear is the immobilizing factor.

Sometimes clients fear violent retaliation or are afraid the spouse will kidnap the children. While these fears may be realistic in some cases, I can point out that some legal safeguards are available. Of course counselors are not equipped to give legal advice, but I recommend that divorce counselors find an attorney specializing in family law so they can consult on legal questions. For example, counselors need to know their state's provisions for restraining orders (to keep separated spouses from harassing), and for grants of temporary custody and support before a dissolution. It is a good idea to have a list available of free or low-cost legal services and other services such as shelters for battered women. I encourage my clients to call the police and to bring charges in case of violence and to take precautions if they fear that the other parent will steal the children. For instance, they can get the cooperation of schools and daycare workers in refusing to let unauthorized individuals pick up the children. Many years ago one of my clients was advised by a police officer to buy a gun and to use it in case her ex-husband came pounding at her door again. When he reappeared, she shot him in the arm in front of her terrified children. I trust that this advice is not universally followed at present, although it did succeed in keeping the angry man away.

In exploring the rationalizations hiding the real fears that paralyze many sufferers, I often find that such people have been living out a passive, victimized role for years, emotionally if not physically battered. For these clients one good approach is to use the victim-rescuer-persecutor triangle described by transactional analysis therapist Claude Steiner in *Scripts People Live* (1964). In this model a victim is a person who seems to want help but makes no effort to help himself or herself; rescuers are people who offer help even if it is not requested and soon find that the victim does not appreciate the aid; rescuers then become resentful and critical of the victim, and move into the persecutor position, or, feeling rejected, become victims themselves. In the meantime, the victims, angry because they cannot get what they want and feeling put down by the offers of help, may begin to persecute the would-be rescuer. And often persecutors, feeling guilty about their anger, become sorry for the victim and may start rescue operations again. Thus anyone who becomes embroiled in the triangle is likely to move from one position to the others. Let this be a warning to counselors who feel the urge to rescue rather than to guide clients to help themselves.

A counselor's natural response to an abused wife's horror story may be to plunge into efforts to help her get out of the situation as fast as possible. But the victim is likely to refuse or sabotage these attempts, leading to frustration if not resentment on the part of the counselor who has been hooked into the futile rescuer position. To avoid this, I recommend working with the client on exploring the pay-offs in the passive, abused victim role. No one would do anything unless there were some rewards. Perhaps the greatest pay-off for victims is that they can place all responsibility for the situation squarely on the spouse. Another reward may be the gaining of sympathy from friends and relatives by playing the "Poor me" game—one of the popular manipulations described by Eric Berne in *Games People Play* (1964). Another game that may fit the situation is the "See how hard I've tried!" ploy. Without blaming, next I try to explore what the victim is doing to possibly perpetuate the abuse. The victim is not actively provoking the maltreatment, but by putting up with it, the sufferer is actually giving the partner reinforcement for continuing. After each episode of insults or beatings, if the victim stays on, there is no incentive for the abuser to stop.

The case of fifty-year-old Matthew is an example. I saw him in treatment for several months as he struggled his way out of the victim role. He and Edith, his wife of twenty-six years, had been separated on and off for two years while she vacillated between wanting a divorce and wanting Matthew. When her affair with another man ended, she came home to Matthew, only to leave and return again several times. Matthew saw himself as the all-forgiving husband who preserved the family at all costs, even though the family consisted of two grown sons with wives and children of their own. In counseling we focused first on the gratifications he was gaining by remaining in the victim role. One reward was his "good guy" image. When I asked him to relax and see what picture came to mind as he thought of himself as a good guy, he described himself as a small boy coming straight home from school and getting praise from mother for helping her around the house. He soon realized that being a good husband while getting no companionship, no cooperation, and no sex was a very thin reward indeed.

Matthew began then to see Edith more realistically as an unloving, self-centered person who was taking advantage of his patience and keeping him in reserve in case her new adventures did not work out. Instead of passively waiting for Edith to make up her mind he was able to take his power back and decided to end his marriage. This step took courage because Matthew suffered from many of the usual fears—he would be criticized, he would hurt his children, he would hurt his parents. To his surprise, his sons agreed with his decision. One said "We thought you'd never see the light." His conservative parents who he assumed would be disgraced by his divorce were actually pleased. Not wanting to interfere, they had not told him they were hoping he would end his unhappy situation. When clients express fear of hurting their parents they are probably more concerned with facing parents' disapproval—clearly an anxiety left over from childhood. Each fear has to be examined rationally. I often ask "What is the disaster that will happen if your parents don't like your decision" or "If you had a son or daughter in the predicament you are now in, what parental advice would you give." To the latter question the answer is often an immediate "I would say, get out of there," or "You have to think of your own happiness." This can help reduce the fear to more manageable proportions. When Matthew finally made a responsible choice he was able to feel more like an adult person. "I feel a lot taller" was the way he described it.

When clients express the fear of being alone, of not being able to make it on their own, or of making a terrible mistake as their reasons for not leaving a destructive marriage, these fears are very likely rationalizations stemming from long-standing dependency needs. I use the transactional analysis model of Parent-Adult-Child ego states to help make the real conflict clear. If people are afraid to stand alone, to take responsibility for their own lives, and to take the consequences of their own decisions, then they are in the fearful Child position like a five-year old venturing out on the first day of school. This is especially true if they have gone straight from the parental home into marriage without a period of making it on their own.

To help clients overcome these fears and achieve a more reasonable Adult position, I ask them to examine the old Parent injunctions. Many fears of independent action stem from old messages from a critical parent—"You're not old enough to do it alone," "Let me do it for you," "See, you made a mistake." Other parent messages may account for the strong shoulds and guilt feelings that surround thoughts of divorce. "Marriages are made in heaven," "What will people think?" and of course "You've made your bed, now lie in it" are some of the parent messages clients have revealed. Some are present-day admonitions from living parents. Others are echoes from old rules.

Injecting reasonable adult beliefs into this mixture of fear and guilt can be a time consuming task. In his books on rational-emotive therapy, Albert Ellis (1977, 1982) suggests replacing "shoulds," "oughts," and "musts," with "It would be better if . . . ," or "I would prefer it if . . ." in order to defuse the power of the old injunctions. To say "I wish that I could stick to my commitment," or "It would be better if I could continue in this marriage" instead of "I ought to stick it out," helps the client see that shoulds and oughts are not unbreakable laws. Exploration of childhood dependence on parental rules may be necessary before clients can see that they are now old enough to make their own rules. Sometimes I say to a client "Right now you are as old as, or older than your mother was when she gave you these messages. Since you are now an adult as old and as wise as she was then, isn't your judgment just as good as hers or better." This can be effective in putting parental injunctions in a less oppressive light.

Another method that has helped people to deal with the fear of being alone is to work on separating survival needs from wants and wishes. Although it is easy to use the word *need* carelessly as a synonym for *want,* there is a great difference between survival needs such as air, food, water, and shelter and wishes for things it would be nice to have. It would be pleasant to have financial security and a good companion rather than being poor and alone. Certainly infants and small children cannot survive without someone to depend on, but do adults have this same need? It may take a good deal of work before a client can accept the rational adult position that one may want the security of another person but a companion is not necessary for survival. Dorothea, who had clung to the belief that any husband was better than none, could not think of giving up her unsatisfying marriage until she had found another man. After many weeks of counseling, one day she slowly said the words herself—"I see it now. I *want* to have a husband, but I don't absolutely *need* one." This was a giant step toward her decision to make it on her own.

Although the women's movement and the gradual improvement in economic opportunities have opened up more options for women who contemplate living on their own, their incomes are still well below those of men. Consciousness raising groups can help women see their own strengths and gain a feeling of solidarity with other women in similar situations. I often refer a client to such a group. Men struggling with loneliness, unfamiliar housework chores, and entertaining children on weekends are finding value in rap groups, sometimes available through churches and YMCAs. Sources for such groups are listed in the Appendix.

It has been my experience that men more often than women put off the decision to divorce until a new romance is waiting in the wings. In our society it is easier for a man to find a woman who is willing to wait for him while he works his way out of his marriage. I have worked in counseling with several of these "other" women. Sometimes the victim-rescuer drama is plain to see. The man may see himself as the victim of a cruel wife and the new woman takes on the role of rescuer. Or the woman may feel like a victim who is unable to find a more appropriate mate so she waits to be rescued by the married man. In either case, a marriage based on rescue operations is not too likely to succeed and may develop the same problems as the previous marriage. If a person needs a safety net before giving up a dysfunctional relationship, it probably means that the old dependency needs have not been resolved and that he or she may not be ready to assume a responsible adult role. Unfortunately, people who have found a new romantic interest are usually so happy that they feel no need to examine their motives and their decisions in counseling.

Sometimes the fear of hurting the partner is the strong reason for not making the break. When this occurs, I ask the client to look closely at what he or she does to the partner by continuing to live there without loving feelings. Even though the spouse begs the client to stay, with or without love, the consequences of staying on can be hurtful to both. The one who stays to avoid hurting the other's feelings will undoubtedly resent the decision and will feel stuck in an empty relationship based on shoulds. "I should never be unkind," "I should never break a promise" are the old injunctions. Soon such a person will be in the victim position, with all its potential for self-pity and angry martyrdom. Bill was obsessed for months about leaving or not leaving his wife, Margery. After twelve years her unsympathetic behavior and incompatible values had destroyed his good feelings for her. Still, he tried to improve the marriage by taking her on excursions and doing the things she wanted done around the house. He became cold and withdrawn, and his only consolation was his belief that he was doing the right thing. He knew that Margery would be deeply hurt if he left but in counseling he began to see that keeping her in this loveless, resentful situation was not being kind to her. He was giving her no real emotional support and was preventing her from finding a new relationship with a more suitable partner. Bill also began to realize that treating Margery as though she could not survive the rejection and make a life for herself was to some extent infantilizing her. Bill had been, in fact, both a victim and a rescuer, neither of which is a fulfilling way to live. Although he was ready to end the marriage, he still had to cope with strong guilt feelings. As we examined the uncomfortable guilt feelings, Bill gradually could see that a good part of his wish to save Margery from hurt was his own wish to rescue himself from guilt.

In the final stage of counseling, Bill learned a new way of looking at guilt. After all, if he could walk out on his wife of twelve years without pangs of guilt, he would not be the considerate kind of person he wanted to be. In a way the guilt made it possible for him to maintain his self-respect at a time when many of his friends and relatives were criticizing him. Bill found that the guilt gradually diminished as he accepted the reasonableness of his decision.

If a client fears that dissolution will cause the rejected mate to commit suicide, the main task for the counselor may be to clarify the issue of taking responsibility for one's own actions. For two people who have lived together for years, the line between their separate responsibilities may have become blurred. A divorce can certainly lead to a great deal of depression, self-blame, and feelings of worthlessness, particularly for the one who did not want it. But no one can be responsible for another adult's chosen behavior. The rejected person may decide to seek help from friends, family, or a therapist, or may choose to put an end to life. In any case, the choice is motivated by a complex of attitudes, perceptions, and impulses, not by the divorce alone. The counselor can help reduce the guilt for the client who initiated the dissolution by emphasizing that the spouse's personality patterns stem from years of conditioning for which the client is not responsible.

If the spouse actually makes a suicide threat, I try to help my client decide whether the threat is real or if it is just a manipulative maneuver designed to prolong the marriage. Since no threats can be lightly dismissed I try to find out if the depressed person has made a definite plan for suicide. Dick came for counseling when he was contemplating divorce from his wife Helen who had been drinking very heavily during the five years of their marriage. Three years ago he had gone with her to a therapist but she had refused to continue treatment. He tried other therapists but when her condition worsened he insisted on taking her to a residential facility for alcoholism treatment. She did not like the place and came home after a few days. In counseling, Dick decided to give her another chance. He chose another treatment center but again Helen remained there for less than a week. Dick attempted to arrange other treatment possibilities that I suggested, all of which she refused. After this, Dick decided he could not tolerate the situation any longer and told Helen that he would have to leave. She did not believe him at first, but when he actually filed for divorce, she threatened to kill herself. She had made such threats before but this time Dick sensed that the threat was serious. He found a bottle of sleeping pills and threw them out. He called Helen's sister to stay with her during the day when he was at work. The next evening when Helen screamed continuously that she was going to do it, he called a crisis clinic for help in having her committed to a mental hospital for her own safety. The next day he made further calls to make the arrangements but it was too late. Helen had hidden another bottle of sleeping pills and had taken them all.

As might be expected after the suicide, Dick was troubled with guilt feelings. To relieve them, we went over the steps that Dick had taken to prevent the irrevocable act. He had searched for the pills, he had evaluated the threat as real, he had alerted other relatives to the danger, and he had taken steps to have Helen committed. It was hard for him to accept the fact that he had done all he could but gradually he stopped criticizing himself for not doing something sooner. He still blamed himself because he had asked for the divorce. Again, we went over all the times he had taken Helen for counseling and all of his efforts to place her in residential treatment. It was clear to me, and finally to Dick, that he had acted responsibly, and that a good, mutually satisfying marriage was simply not possible. It was difficult for Dick to come to the conclusion that it was up to Helen to cope with the break up and that the unfortunate choice of ending her life was not the only one available. I continually reminded Dick that he had done everything that was available at the time, and that no one can make another person do anything. I asked Dick to imagine staying in the marriage in order to keep Helen alive. This would have been a rescue operation, with all the resentment that goes with it, and not a cooperative, loving relationship. Dick's guilt gradually faded as his self-blame was reduced and he accepted a certain amount of remorse as natural in such a tragedy.

If religious beliefs are the basis for hesitating to end a destructive marriage, I proceed cautiously. Sometimes the religious injunctions are a rationalization for the basic fears of being criticized and being left alone. But if the religious person is seriously concerned with not breaking a religious credo, the counselor can explore the beliefs and the feelings they arouse. Even though the client's church may frown on divorce, the counselor may point out that most Christian groups and many other religions see God as more compassionate than punishing. If the client can see that the marriage was a mistake, he or she may be able to accept the idea that a deity would not want anyone to endure years of misery as punishment for one mistake. For one client the turning point came when he at last realized that he was being harder on himself than his god would be. Since he believed that God forgave sinners he eventually was able to forgive himself for ending his marriage.

Having at last decided on dissolution, an individual may find it very hard to break the news to the partner who wants to preserve the union. Jeannette, who had been in individual treatment, asked me to be present at the actual moment she conveyed her decision to Don, her husband. I had seen Don in marital therapy with Jeannette the previous year. Jeannette felt safer and stronger in my presence and wanted Don to have the empathy she knew I could give as he received the wound. Jeannette found that her task was easier than she expected but the meeting was a very tearful scene. Both cried. Don fought against the decision at first, but by the end of the hour, accepted the inevitable. Jeannette continued in counseling as she planned her new life. Don recovered with remarkable ease and was remarried not long after the divorce.

With another couple, the scene was violent as the husband screamed and begged his wife on his knees not to leave. When she was adamant, he dashed out of the room, cut his arm with a razor blade, then ran to the parking lot to drip blood on her car. A quick call to the police and the medical aid car took care of this unfortunate man. A follow-up call a few days later satisfied me that he had become calmer and was reconciled to the separation. His request for a joint appointment had been a last ditch attempt to forestall a break. Neither one chose to come in for further counseling.

Unmarried couples living together also come for help when deciding on separation. If they have lived together for a number of years with a strong commitment their decision on whether to keep or break the relationship can be as difficult as that of a married couple. Several books have been written by lawyers about the legal and financial pitfalls of living together without marriage. I have not yet seen much psychological research on the problems of living together or on ending such a relationship. The pain can certainly be as wrenching as in a divorce and the social supports can be less substantial. Family and friends are likely to feel less involved and less needed. Furthermore, without the definite end point a dissolution decree signifies, the separating couple may have a harder time giving up the attachment and the hope of a reconciliation. Thus a rejected person may be stuck longer in a state of limbo, unwilling to accept the finality of the separation. Even if the former partner goes to live with another person, this is not as final an ending as the remarriage of a former spouse. After all, since the old relationship was not permanent, it may be hard to accept the permanence of the new one.

On the other hand, I have seen several individuals who married after having a satisfactory living together arrangement, then separated and divorced not long after the wedding. Doreen and Alan had lived together for two years. Their relationship had been so good they decided to marry. They stayed in the same apartment and their lives followed the same routine, but for Alan there was a subtle change. He confessed that "I used to come home because I wanted to; now I know I have to come home to Doreen and I feel trapped." Alan began to explore this coerced feeling in counseling but he soon admitted that having to change his view of things made him feel all the more trapped. Apparently Alan was unrealistically perceiving himself as a victim but he did not wish to continue in counseling. The marriage soon broke up, leaving Doreen with a good deal of despondency that she continued to deal with in counseling.

A similar young couple, Donna and Bob, lived happily together for three years but her parents who lived at the opposite end of the country were critical of the unconventional arrangement. Their attitude did not deter Donna until her parents planned to visit. Eager to please them, Donna decided it would be appropriate for her and Bob to get married as a highlight of the visit. Bob was a compliant fellow and did not think that marriage would upset the relationship. A few months later it became clear that Donna was not just appeasing her parents by marrying but rescuing herself from some unpleasant guilt feelings. Soon after the wedding when the pair had disagreements, feelings of resentment toward the parents and toward each other for catering to parents' wishes began to surface, and the marriage did not last long. The couple did not seek counseling at the time, but I saw Donna two years later for other problems and she told of the short-lived marriage. Had I seen them in counseling before the dissolution we no doubt would have had to address issues of dependency and of taking responsibility for one's own decisions.

While most of the dissolutions I have seen have not been occasions for happiness, George Bach, the psychiatrist who coauthored *The Intimate Enemy* (1968), has suggested an "unwedding ceremony" to mark a dignified end to a relationship. He has reported on several such events, which usually take place when both partners are taking part in a marathon or long-term therapy group. (See his chapter "Creative Exits" in *Women in Therapy* by Franks and Burtle 1974.) Friends are gathered around, as at a wedding, and the couple share in a solemn goodbye ritual.

Rabbi Grollman has also invented a divorce ceremony designed to end a marriage with dignity and consideration (Grollman and Sams 1978). He points out that all other life milestones are marked by rituals, which not only punctuate transitions, but provide an opportunity for closure. His ceremony includes a discussion of the earlier commitment, the growing apart, the impossibility of continuing together, and a renewed commitment by both to function together as parents to their children. He finds that the ritual helps children to accept their parents' divorce. Relatives are asked to be present, and as one might expect, tears are shed. Perhaps these valuable ceremonies will become more common in the future, but in my work with torn apart couples the great emotional turmoil on both sides usually means that a calm and constructive meeting at the end of the marriage is not possible for everyone.

Whether a couple comes in together, vacillating about preserving their marriage or going their separate ways, or whether an individual comes in alone, trying to decide on taking the momentous step, I find that no one method is best for all cases. The main aim is to help the struggling clients uncover and articulate their real wishes and attitudes so that they will make choices on the basis of life values important to them. Equally important is exploring their fears of making changes, and sorting out the realistic from the unrealistic anxieties. As I have pointed out, the counselor can challenge irrational ideas through cognitive methods, can clarify the well learned habits through dynamic or transactional analysis techniques, and can bring about changes in behavior through gestalt methods, trial separations, and other exercises. Once the decision to divorce has been made, whether or not it is a constructive one, the counselor moves on to the next task that might be called "picking up the pieces."

4
Practical Problems

Once an individual has decided to divorce, or divorce has been thrust upon him or her, some practical problems must be solved at once. Whether clients have suffered through months of weighing the alternatives or the decision has been sudden, the actual event is a step into a strange new world. In the midst of the emotional wrench of ending a marriage no one is in the best shape to make practical decisions about financial and housing arrangements. First, the couple must consider which person will remain in the family home and which will move out. If they own a house they must decide if the house should be sold, and furniture and other assets must be divided. If the parent without the responsibility for housing the children moves out, he or she may have trouble finding quarters large enough for the children's visits. Often sons and daughters must bring sleeping bags and bed down on the floor of a small apartment. If the parent with the children must move it is likely to be to a lower rent neighborhood, away from friends, schools, churches, and other supports.

Unless the couple has excellent financial resources there will not be enough money. Spreading the available income over two households can make a thin layer for each. Many times I have heard women complain that the support money is not enough while men complain that after they pay support they do not have enough left to live on. While counselors are not trained to be financial advisers, I recommend that they become familiar with the financial facts of life faced by families in dissolution. Lenore Weitzman studied 3,000 California families and reports in *The Divorce Revolution: The Unexpected Social and Economic Consequences for Women and Children in America* (1985) that after dissolution the women and children suffered a 73 percent drop in their standard of living whereas the men's rose 42 percent. While many fathers will protest this, the average support payment is no more than $2,000 a year and 40 percent of departed parents contribute nothing at all to their families. Even if a mother has custody of several children, the father is very rarely expected to give as much as half of his income to the custodial parent and payments tend to disappear after several years. When a court orders a man to pay up on defaulted payments he may fail to do so. Even if he is conscientious in providing support, a father is not as likely to be in such a financial bind as his ex-wife and children. He may be further advanced in his career and less in need of further education. He may have better knowledge of the family's assets and may be better able to afford an experienced attorney to work on his behalf. He may be able to arrange for helpful affidavits, psychological evaluations, and other legal investigations that will gain him an advantage in the divorce settlement.

Since support payments are rarely sufficient for a family to live on, the custodial parent will often have to supplement the amount with Aid to Families with Dependent Children funds or by getting a job. Since women on the average earn only sixty cents for every dollar earned by a man, their total income can still be far below that of an ex-husband. Working means finding child care, another expense for custodial parents. Our government and business policies do not give high priority to funding daycare centers and enforcing high standards, so that many single parents must resort to unlicensed private homes of poor quality, or leave children alone after school and during vacations.

Procedures vary from state to state for recovering missing support payments. A recent federal law provides for the Internal Revenue Service to withhold support payments from income tax refunds but only after all state and local efforts have been unsuccessful. In some cases the state may collect and disburse the payments. When fathers have custody, if the mother is working or has other income, she may have to contribute support. Knowing the available resources will help a counselor distinguish between a person who is genuinely unable to get a support order enforced and one who is adopting the victim role and blaming the ex-spouse, instead of doing everything possible to collect.

Alimony is rarely granted at present since women are usually considered capable of supporting themselves. Support for an ex-wife is called maintenance and may be granted for a limited time. In awarding it, the judge may consider the financial resources available, the woman's ability to support herself, and the length of time necessary for her to acquire job training. The position of a woman married for twenty-five or more years, who has raised a family and never worked outside the home, can be very precarious in a dissolution. Job possibilities for a woman of fifty-five with no work experience are limited. I have occasionally testified in court on behalf of such a woman whose lack of education or severe emotional problems make it unlikely that she can compete in the job market.

One woman client was required to go to college for business training as a condition for her maintenance payments. She was told that she must go to summer school as well but she was able to get this part of the order changed by an understanding judge who recognized her need for respite and time to be with her adolescent children. It is only fair, of course, if the wife is much wealthier than the husband, that she be required to give him maintenance. This happens occasionally.

In recent years the problems of women who have served society by raising children, assisting in their husbands' careers, and taking care of a home have been heeded by our federal and some state governments. These divorced or widowed women have been dignified with the title "displaced homemakers." Service centers for them have been set up, usually in community colleges. A national Displaced Homemakers Network keeps the local agencies in touch with legislation, conferences, and relevant reading material. The centers provide not only job counseling and job readiness programs, but support groups, legal, financial, and health advice, and referrals to other agencies helpful to women newly on their own. Unfortunately there have been severe cutbacks in federal funds since 1981 and the success of these centers will depend on finding other sources of funding since the services are usually free.

A similar kind of facility for women called the Women's Guidance Center was established at the University of Washington in the early 1970s in order to meet the needs of the many women returning to college after years of homemaking. The Center offered courses on choosing careers and preparing to enter the job market as well as individual counseling on academic and vocational choices. For several years I taught a course entitled Divorce, Before and After, which was added to the curriculum since divorce problems kept intruding into the discussions on careers. These classes showed me that group discussion is definitely the method of choice for dealing with the practical problems of divorce.

While they were listed as classes, my groups resembled group therapy more than academic courses. I have used group psychotherapy for years as a powerful method of treatment for emotional problems. A counselor may not wish to be directive or advice-giving with an individual client even though the client may desperately need guidance. A group of peers freely shares advice and can suggest many more alternatives than one counselor can. Many peer suggestions have been tested successfully. Groups also give good opportunities for criticisms and modifications of the various recommendations.

There was no intention to discriminate against men in my classes and men were later included in all the programs. (Funding cuts eventually eliminated the Guidance Center.) There are advantages to mixed groups—men and women can become more understanding of the problems faced by one another in dissolution. One-sex groups have other values—women, especially in groups led by a woman counselor, can more freely share and empathize with one another and can be very open about intimate matters. Men, too, may feel more free to open up with other men than in a mixed group.

My groups consisted of women who had been recently divorced, some who were still struggling to adjust after one or two years, and several who were contemplating divorce. The ages ranged from the twenties through the sixties. Some of the marriages had lasted more than twenty-five years, and most had produced children. The first meeting of each class had a heavy atmosphere—members looked at each other cautiously and were reluctant to reveal much information about themselves. I usually began with a short talk about one of the various problems faced in divorce. The stiff faces began to relax as these anxious people saw that I had some understanding of what they were going through. I find that in every group there is someone who is willing to begin the discussion and then others will continue it. I always arrange the chairs in a circle rather than in rows. With the leader in the circle, rather than in front, people are more likely to direct remarks to each other rather than to the authority figure.

Not all clinicians can use the group method. Training in group facilitation, if not group psychotherapy, is essential. I see the counselor's role as a catalyst—to encourage expression of thoughts and feelings and to stimulate interaction. Instead of asking direct questions it is more productive for the leader to observe and comment on what is going on. For example, I might say, "I noticed that several of us laughed when Dorothy was telling her story." Such an observation may bring out more expressions of feeling than a direct "why" question. The leader can play any hunches suggested by the material. For instance, saying "I noticed that everyone was silent after Lois described her experience. I wonder if that touched off some sad memories" is likely to stimulate someone to either confirm or deny the hunch. It is tempting for a counselor to respond right away to a member's statement or question without waiting for the group members to speak, but this diminishes some of the greatest values of group discussion—the opportunity for people to grow by helping one another and to discover that others have the same problems.

Money problems, a concern for most divorcing people, inevitably came up in the discussions. Groups can reveal a remarkable range of talents for earning and saving money. My groups also shared their philosophies about money. One member pointed out that some spending is not really spending, but investing. Money spent for education, for example, is an investment that will yield dividends for many years, not only in financial terms but in enriched enjoyment of life. Another woman pointed out that counseling is an investment, not a luxury. If it increases self-confidence and reduces anxiety, the rewards can include better relations with people and even greater earning power. Another advantage of group therapy at the time of divorce is that it costs less than individual sessions. Several women shared their knowledge of the local low-cost mental health clinics.

One practical woman refuted the claims of those who insisted that they never could go out because they could not afford babysitters. She insisted that the cost of sitters is also an investment in oneself that will yield new social life, a better disposition, and possibly connections that will help in a job search. Another experienced job hunter said that she had invested in a new suit and a professional hairdo before an important job interview because it gave her a better self-image and more confidence. All of these suggestions pointed to the often overlooked value of psychological income. After all, what is money for if not to promote emotional well being?

Some members had borrowed money for their college tuition and for other necessities such as a refrigerator. Having to make monthly payments helped to structure the budget and gave incentive to search for ways to earn money. One woman was considering an ingenious method of savings she had read about in a magazine. She planned to persuade a bank to lend her a thousand dollars just to put in a savings account. She would pay off the loan in small monthly amounts and would have the savings always available for emergencies. In the end she would "own" the thousand dollars. "That's the only way I can force myself to save," she confessed.

Turning to budget problems, my groups came up with many remarkable ways of saving money. People exchanged addresses of places to buy used clothing and day-old bread. As one bargain hunter pointed out, "Bread is a day old the day after you buy it." They shared experiences at low-cost medical clinics, free entertainment at city parks and libraries, and low-cost haircuts at beauty schools. Many of the women had never had to think of such ways of economizing before.

Those women who were in the midst of deciding on dissolution found a good deal of practical help in the suggestions and mistakes of those who had been through the process. The veterans told the others how to make a budget that would include not only necessities but also a fund for unforeseen expenses such as repairs to shoes, automobiles, and houses. This helped the inexperienced predict how much they would need to live on their own. Having the husband continue the childrens' medical insurance and putting charge accounts in the women's own names, as well as including a cost-of-living escalation clause in the support agreement, were important bits of advice. In the early 1970s divorced women were often denied charge accounts even if they held good jobs. The groups were helpful in checking out stores that did not discriminate in this way and in finding agencies that could help with discrimination problems. I received a good education about the various organizations that can serve divorced people. Some of these are listed in the Appendix.

Whether or not to sell the family home is another troubling decision that came up in the groups. No general rules apply, but those who had resolved the problem offered their experiences, including advice about real estate agents and books to read on the subject. For those women who were forced to move, discussion of the pros and cons of owning versus renting a home was helpful. Many of the women had never had to face such decisions on their own. Ingrid, a woman with a large house and a small income offered an interesting solution. She took in a couple of roomers and found that this not only brought in income but reduced her feelings of isolation. This appealed to me as a sensible idea but at first several of the women were very uncomfortable with it. A client's perception of roomers may be quite unsavory—a step down in the world. At the very least a stranger in the house seemed to some like an unwelcome intrusion. Had I made a similar suggestion in individual counseling, it might not have been accepted. But in a group these negative perceptions are more likely to change as happened after Ingrid described her experience. Jean, who had rented a room to a college student, had an arrangement that provided her with a built-in babysitter. Another woman brought up the old saying "A stranger is a friend you haven't met." Ingrid told how she and the roomers had maintained privacy. Rules about the use of the shared kitchen and living room had worked out well. She also described her ways of interviewing and screening prospective renters. She had advertised only at the university and in a newspaper that appealed to educated people. Gertrude was skeptical at first about renting a room but then she began to like the idea of having someone who would do babysitting and other chores. She also realized that she would feel safer with another adult in the house in case of emergencies.

In exploring ways of making money, the women uncovered many ideas for putting their talents to work at home. Some who had had no job experience outside their homes found that their homemaking abilities had economic value. One woman who loved to give parties began to think about catering cocktail parties and other special events. Another looked into telephoning jobs and shared her experience about how to judge them. Some warned against addressing envelopes at home because of the very unreliable income. Priscilla, who had two small children and a roomy house, was already making plans to offer daycare. "Since I want to be home with my own children, I might as well have a few more for them to play with," she said. Some of the women found typing or bookkeeping at home were good possibilities.

As for jobs outside the home, the excellent wages for women in nontraditional occupations such as electrician, mechanic, or painter surprised many who had never thought of such a career. Dorothy looked into the training programs for several of these occupations and reported back to the group. Several who had thought that secretarial jobs were their only option investigated offerings at vocational schools. Others signed up for career orientation courses at the university to learn about other unconventional job possibilities. Some took advantage of the vocational aptitude testing offered by the university and the local community colleges to find out what fields might be most appropriate for them. Exchanging information about courses they had taken, workshops they attended, and agencies that had given good career guidance broadened the women's knowledge. Unless counselors are trained in career counseling, it is important for them to know where to refer clients for this specialized kind of help. Eloise surprised everyone by joining the Army Reserves. By giving a few weekends and evenings and two weeks in the summer, she could earn a significant amount without taking too much time away from her children.

Inevitably the group members discussed the perennial problem of how to get support payments from lagging fathers, and their difficulties with visitations. They exchanged information about legal procedures and costs, and exchanged names of lawyers who had been helpful and sympathetic and those who had not. Women who had used the do-it-yourself process pointed out the pitfalls of this method unless a couple has few assets and no children. The combined knowledge of a group will very likely be greater than that of a counselor who may never have had to consult a lawyer at all. Inviting an attorney or a family court worker to speak to the group and to answer general questions turned out to be a good way to clear up some of the confusion about legal matters. If there is a divorce mediation service available, this is another good resource for those who have not yet reached a dissolution agreement.

The groups were very helpful in finding child care. They gave each other leads on how to find good caregivers, and discussed the relative merits of old and young sitters. Some members had placed ads in supermarkets and some had contacted local high schools and colleges. Verna had been part of a child care cooperative where parents saved money by taking care of one another's offspring in the neighborhood. They took turns keeping track of hours spent so that each co-op member would receive as many hours as she or he put in. Verna reported that the system worked well. "I found it was easier to get other people's children into bed than my own," she said with a laugh. One father, a graduate student, liked sitting in other people's houses in the evening. He told Verna that he could study in peace; at home his wife kept talking to him. Verna pointed out that a co-op would be more difficult to arrange with single parents. They would have to take their own youngsters along to the neighbor's home, or do their share of contributing when their children were in school or away visiting father or other relatives.

One of the greatest values of the group method is that members can assign one another homework and check up on the results. A shy member might be given the task of going for one job interview before the next week's meeting even if the chances of being hired are poor, the purpose being to "get her feet wet" in the strange new world of job hunting. Sure that the member must face the group's disapproval if she fails in her task gives incentive for her to go. When she returns to the group with her assignment accomplished she receives positive reinforcement and a little more confidence for her next interview.

Lucile, who realized that she would have to take some business training, procrastinated on the grounds that she had no idea of which business school to choose or whether the community college courses would be preferable. This indecision saved her from facing the fact that she was really on her own—no longer a housewife—a situation she deplored at every meeting. The group did not accept Lucile's excuses for long and insisted on action. Since Lucile had no idea how much the schools charged or what courses they offered, she was given the simple assignment of going to two of the institutions and getting their catalogs. When she turned up the next week with only one catalog and several poor excuses, group members confronted her with her reluctance to start on her new life and pointed out that she was playing the "Yes, but" game described by Berne (1964). Their tough approach pushed Lucile to take the necessary steps toward accepting the reality of her new situation.

All too often my groups resorted to playing similar games, all of which are transactions with ulterior motives rather than straight factual communications. At the time of divorce, people can play "Ain't it awful?" by exchanging horror stories about their miserable experiences. The pay-off is not great, but apparently attractive. There is some gratification in proving to others that one is blameless, a feeling of superiority if one's tale of abuse tops the others'. Meg seized center stage with a really dramatic episode—"Would you believe I went back in the house one day and found him in *my* bed with that woman?" If the game is identified the clients can learn in a humorous, nonthreatening way what they are doing. They can evaluate the cheap rewards and get back on the track of more constructive problem solving.

Playing "Poor me" is very tempting for people in the midst of a painful divorce. "He left me without a cent," or "I can't even buy shoes for the children," or "She cleaned me out" are typical examples of "Poor me." A good way to counteract this game is to ask the client to describe the unhappy situation in detail, and to say "Poor me!" loud and clear after each sentence. This exercise will soon stop the game as the player is embarrassed to see the group's sympathy change to disgust and then to laughter.

"Wooden Leg" is another favorite of the newly divorced and divorcing. The name comes from the story of a man with a wooden leg who refused to work or do anything to help himself, saying "What can you expect from a man with a wooden leg?" This game often turns up as an excuse for not finding a job. Some of the versions I have heard are "I can't get a job because I haven't any training," or "I can't go back to school because I'm too old," or "I'm too fat to get the kind of job I'd like—they'd never hire me," or "They're prejudiced against divorced people—they find excuses for not hiring us." The game not only protects the player from risky ventures but displaces responsibility for one's life on to the rest of the world. Thus the difficult task of creating a new life is postponed or avoided. Groups can easily spot games and help one another to avoid them. In dealing with these games it is important to keep the focus away from complaints about the past, and to constantly point the clients in the direction of the future and its possibilities.

Practical Problems • 53

Some of the group members who had been through the experience of dissolution helped to focus on the future by giving reassurance and realistic advice to those who were standing on the brink of divorce. Those who had made the break could give a detailed map of the territory ahead and thus help uncertain members decide whether or not to leave their marriage. Members can bring in and share books, magazine articles and lists of agencies useful in coping with dissolution. Every week the women in my groups brought in relevant newspaper clippings and data about community organizations of interest to newly single people. And finally, beside the mutual benefits from shared financial and other concerns, the women gave one another a good deal of support on finding social life and fun again.

At the end of a series of group sessions, I recommend that the participants fill out an evaluation sheet. Questions such as the following will help the leader plan for the next group.

What did you like best about the group?

What did you think should be changed or improved?

Was the discussion too personal or not personal enough?

Were topics important to you omitted?

Would you have preferred more reading and reporting assignments?

Did the leader exercise too much control or not enough?

Did you think that the situations of the members were too different?

Did you think there was too much similarity in viewpoints?

These are suggestions. A leader can devise a more highly structured evaluation form with quantitative results. With one group, I asked each woman to draw a picture of herself at the beginning, and again after the last of the six-week series of meetings. These results were interesting in that some of the people appeared happier in the second drawing, and one, perhaps more aware of the realities of divorce, looked sadder. While my groups gave the members a good deal of emotional support and sometimes insight, I would recommend that people who are having serious emotional difficulties take part in psychotherapy groups rather than classes where the emphasis is on the more practical concerns.

One of the best outcomes of the group method I have described was that the participants soon realized that the others were nice people like themselves. Gradually they learned that being divorced was not as odious as they had thought and that it can happen to anyone. I saw a remarkable contrast between the stiffness of the first meeting when many were ashamed of their situation and reluctant to discuss it, and the relaxed atmosphere of the final sessions. One group, at the end of the course, adjourned to a restaurant to enjoy a drink and some jazz music together. Another group decided to meet on their own after the class ended. Some members became good friends and continued to be supportive of one another.

5
The Stress of Changing Roles

While both men and women are usually aware that financial and practical problems will follow if they decide to divorce, they are often less aware of the inevitable role changes that will also occur. Our sense of identity, of being an acceptable person, usually develops from our various roles. As in a play, our role in life often determines much of our behavior. Playing an unimportant servant role in a drama is not as varied and fulfilling as playing the lead, and people who assume or are assigned life roles they believe are insignificant will act in character and will have a diminished sense of identity and self-esteem. We do not have a rigid caste or class system in this country but we are all cast as men or women, young or old, married or not, and our economic status and our place in the world of work also determine our roles to a large extent.

The roles we take on early in life can have a profound effect on our self-image and confidence. The transactional analysis life script concept described by Steiner (1964) emphasizes how we keep acting in our childhood roles until therapy or a significant life change leads us to learn new life scripts. A youngest child, for example, may spend a lifetime acting out the role of the helpless little one who needs lots of attention. Another person may feel important and confident as an adult because he was trusted as a child with babysitting younger brothers. A boy who was guarded with sitters until high school years is likely to feel the opposite.

Later experiences as well as childhood can influence the life script. A person who has learned to fill a variety of interesting roles will have a good chance of developing a secure self-image. A woman who can function well as daughter, mother, wife, teacher, church worker, and soccer player has more sources of self-acceptance than does one who takes on no role other than housewife, or who sees herself as nothing but a businesswoman. A single role is more vulnerable.

A definite ritual marks and validates the change of role from married person to widow or widower. The funeral ceremony, the flowers, letters of sympathy, offerings of food, and other kindnesses from relatives and friends ease the painful passage to the new status. But no such rituals accompany a dissolution. A businesslike interview in an attorney's office and a cold, unpleasant formality in a courtroom are the only ceremonies, and suddenly the two people have taken on a new life role—they are divorced.

Some see their new status as a sudden drop from success to failure. Society places high value on marriage and it is a respected goal for both men and women. With the lingering aura of imperfection, if not evil, that still clings to the word *divorce,* not surprisingly many divorced people feel that they have failed in life. They had planned to stay together and never separate, and no matter what the circumstances, when their dissolution finally becomes public, they may feel so defeated that they find it hard to face the world. Howard, whose wife had left him for another man, described it vividly. Soon after his divorce he went to an evening lecture, sat in the back row, and left quickly at the end even though friends he usually liked to chat with were in the audience.

Even the name for the new status is problematical. Ex-wife and ex-husband have a negative connotation. Women are called divorcees, but men have no comparable label. However, men keep their original names. A woman is no longer Mrs. John Jones. She is now Mrs. or Ms. Elizabeth Jones unless she resumes her maiden name. Some women have used their original surname for a first name becoming Mrs. Johnson Jones, for example, which of course suggests their wish to hide their newly single state. A woman with children may hate to keep the former husband's name, but will hesitate to use her maiden name because of the resulting confusion for her children and their schools. The change of name can be a perpetual reminder of failure for a woman who perceives her identity in this way. I am reminded of the subtitle of an old melodrama about a fallen woman—she was described as "Neither Maid, Wife, nor Widow." In the same way, a divorced woman is defined more by what she is not than by what she is. Some may shun her as a fallen woman, but who ever heard of a fallen man, except when he has fallen in love?

Both men and women will more likely see themselves as failures if their self-image and stress tolerance were low to begin with, or if they are part of a social or religious group that frowns on divorce. Counselors can explore the clients' family and social connections to help them see how their identity stems in part from the groups of which they are members. For an older woman who has accepted the traditional role of housewife and whose entire life has revolved around her husband, the role change is particularly hard. She has seen herself as "Mrs. Doctor" or "Joe's wife" for thirty years, and if the welfare of her husband and children was her only career, she may feel that she has no role in life at all when they are gone. Our roles confer meaning, and as Victor Frankl has pointed out, without meaning in life, we feel despair.

The work of the counselor will consist in guiding the client to change this unsatisfactory self-image. Cognitive methods can lessen the failure stigma. Exaggeration may point out the distorted thinking that makes divorced people discount themselves. For example, you might say "Then do you mean that all those thousands of single and divorced people out there are failures because they have no partners? And that all married people, happy or not, are real successes?" Or you can ask "If you had never married, what would you be doing today? What good ways to live would you find? What valuable traits would you have? Would you be hiding from the world?" Or the counselor can dispute failure-ridden thinking by pointing out "You are the same person now that you were last year when you were married. Does the kind of person you are change because your former spouse is no longer with you?" Or "Will you explain to me how the divorce decree can make you into a less acceptable person?" Chances are this will help the client realize that another person's actions, no matter how unpleasant, cannot force anyone to choose the failure role. Many clients are very vulnerable to what others say about divorce or what they imagine others are saying. To work toward the reasonable belief that the clients' own behavior and attitudes create their identity, I might say "You mean the words that come out of another person's mouth can actually change you into a different kind of person?"

Family members are often the first to hear of the dissolution and their reactions will certainly affect the divorced person's role in the family. Parents may be highly supportive, offering a refuge for a divorced son or daughter, which can be excellent emergency shelter for a short time. Other parents, eager to be helpful, may see their divorced offspring as a returning child and treat their adult child so solicitously that they delay independent action. Parents who disapproved of the marriage may welcome the divorce and say "We told you so." If the divorced person feels unhappy and regretful, this parental celebrating will hardly be helpful. Other family members may be so critical that they close ranks against the one who has made the mistake and thrust that person into an outsider role in the family group. Or if some relatives approve and some do not, the perpetrator of the divorce may feel like a troublemaker who stirs up family conflict, certainly not a comfortable role.

Relationships with ex-in-laws and other members of the former spouse's family are likely to be even more complicated. Is the divorced person still a member of the ex-partner's family or not? No guidelines clarify this ambiguous situation. If the relationship was not warm during the marriage, it will no doubt be even cooler after the marriage ends. Even if it was warm, some parents in effect disown the former son- or daughter-in-law. Lila, an only child whose parents were deceased, had enjoyed being part of her husband's large family. After her divorce she missed the family activities and felt very lonely. She described her shock at suddenly finding herself in an entirely different role—"Before I was an in-law; now I seem to be an out-law."

Some parents continue to love the divorced son- or daughter-in-law, but feel torn between that love and their continuing love and loyalty to their own offspring. In this case the "ex" is not an outlaw, but feels a subtle change. She is no longer a real part of family and holiday celebrations and no longer visited as often as before. One mother-in-law continued her caring relationship with her son's former wife as well as with her remarried son and with two sets of grandchildren, but said that she simply could not visit the two households on the same day. She had to allow for some space in between.

Dissolution also brings about a new relationship between children and their grandparents. After a bitter and resentful divorce some people may wish to cut off all connection with the ex-spouse's parents even though they had been good to the children in the past. Such people insist so strongly on their new independent role that they overlook the fact that the children are forever related to their grandmother and grandfather whose interest and caring can be very valuable. Other parents may wish to keep the children's contacts with grandma and grandpa unchanged. Ethel, one of my divorced clients, continued to enjoy her mother-in-law who still was a willing babysitter for her two grandchildren. The two women got along amicably by simply avoiding the subject of the ex-husband. Ethel reported though that the big hole in the conversation was conspicuous, so that neither woman could be completely relaxed as they skirted around the subject and concentrated their talk on the mutually acceptable topic of the children.

Counselors may work with clients who are afraid of becoming ex-grandparents. Mrs. Benson came to me for counseling when her recently divorced son John wanted to oust her from her grandmother role. During the seven years of John's marriage to Althea, Mrs. Benson had grown fond of Althea's two small daughters by a previous marriage and considered them her real grandchildren—she had no others. However, after a very hostile divorce John had no further interest in his stepchildren. When Mrs. Benson invited Althea and the girls to her house to celebrate the older child's birthday, John was enraged. He interpreted his mother's action as disloyalty. Mrs. Benson, who had stayed out of the marital conflicts, had a cordial if not close relationship with Althea, and wanted to solve the dilemma of how to see her granddaughters without antagonizing John. In counseling she was able to sort out her attitudes and see that divorce did not lessen her love for her son or for her grandchildren, and that the grandmother role she wished to play was her choice, not John's. I helped her see that John had a right to cut himself off from Althea and her children but that he could not dictate her behavior toward them. She also saw that she and the children all benefitted from her continued involvement and that she was not trying to hurt her son. Gradually she let go of her guilt and quit feeling responsible for John's anger. Instead she began to understand how John was enraging himself by trying to control her. This did not improve her relationship with John who needed time to recover from the turmoil of divorce, but it allowed her to continue enjoying her occasional visits with her grandchildren.

Mrs. Benson is not the only grandmother who wishes to continue in her role after a dissolution in the family. Some grandparents have sued for and won visitation rights. Fortunately some judges recognize the value of interested grandparents and of family ties in the lives of children whose parents have separated. There is even an organization of grandparents who support each other in their attempts to win contacts with their grandchildren and sometimes even custody. In similar controversial cases, counselors can suggest that grandparents explore the possibility of including their right to visit in the dissolution decree.

An even more disturbing role change occurs in the divorcing person's social network. For some, their first problem is how to notify friends about the dissolution. Divorce announcement cards are on the market but apparently have not achieved any great popularity, and people who are ashamed of divorce do not casually remark "Oh, by the way, Betty and I are divorced." They are more likely to wait until the grapevine has spread the news. When no mention is made, friends may hesitate to bring it up. Thus the lonely single person may get no friendly support. Even when the news is out in the open, friends may feel awkward. Should they express condolence for this sad event or congratulations that an unhappy marriage is over at last? Would it be sympathetic or prying to ask questions? Because we have no rules of divorce etiquette, friends may avoid the divorced person when a helping hand is most needed.

If the social circle consisted entirely of couples, there is now a "fifth wheel" who does not fit in. Couples face still another awkward problem—do they remain loyal to both husband and wife, arranging to see each separately or do they stay friends with one and drop the other entirely? When couples include the newly single person in social events it may be painfully clear that there is an uneven number at the dinner table, and that making conversation is not as easy as before. As time goes on, the interests and activities of couples and singles diverge and the divorced one may fade out of the network. Forty-year-old Florence's introduction to single life was more sudden and traumatic. Since her husband was prominent in local politics, they had been involved for years in a round of dinners and gala events with a large group of coupled friends. Florence had enjoyed entertaining these people and was famous for her elaborate buffet suppers. She stayed in their house after the marriage broke up and found herself sitting alone every weekend. It did not take her long to realize that her friends accepted her only because she was attached to her husband. Her busy social life during the marriage had prevented her from spending time on her own activities and developing separate friendships based on common interests. In counseling she had to get over her anger and disillusionment before she could begin to build a new network for herself.

The rejection by Florence's so-called friends is extreme—friends can vary tremendously in their treatment of the divorced. Some couples do not want to be reminded that divorce can happen to anyone. One overly cautious husband insisted that his wife no longer see a recently separated woman friend, fearing it would give her ideas. Naturally his insistence backfired and gave his wife more ideas about leaving him than if he had been less controlling. Some couples may wish to be helpful but may soon tire of listening to the divorcee's complaints and bitterness. Other friends may be so helpful that the divorced person feels like a pitied invalid.

Some well-meaning friends may thrust blind dates on divorced friends, thinking they need to be paired up with other single people. Ella described her uneasiness about attending a party where she and a strange man were supposed to be a couple. The matchmaking made her uncomfortable because it meant that she was considered incomplete without a partner, a feeling that was compounded when she discovered that she and the man had nothing in common. He scarcely spoke and probably felt as awkward as Ella. This kind of forced pairing can be another unwelcome role change after a dissolution.

After dropping out of the couples' network, a divorced person may still wish to see and enjoy same-sex married friends. A really close friendship may not be affected by the divorce but some of my clients have reported that they experienced a subtle change. One woman described a typical event. She had been chatting on the telephone with her good friend who invited her for dinner. "My husband is going to be out of town," said the friend. My client accepted the invitation, but wondered if she had become a threat to her friend's marriage, or just a handy sitter for a lonely wife. If a wife does feel threatened by an unmarried friend who may be attractive to her husband this will widen the gap between the two women. On the other hand, wives have no such problem inviting single men to their homes—in fact, hostesses prize them.

People may be unhappily aware that they are no longer part of a couples' community but may be unable to accept their new single role. They may not see themselves as part of the singles population. Those who have been married for years may have stopped seeing single friends and may live in a neighborhood consisting entirely of families. Some try for a long time to deny that they are single. Counseling can help them change this denial into acceptance of the reality of their new role. Some clients require a good deal of work before they can see singles as ordinary people.

Group therapy can help change distorted attitudes toward single people. Terry, a stylish young woman, hated to be identified as a single person. "They're dowdy" she complained. "They're losers and everybody knows that they just aren't attractive enough to find or keep a partner." Ed agreed—"That applies to men, too. They just couldn't make it." This started a lively group argument. Fay, who was usually quiet, disagreed energetically—

"That's not true. Most single people are fast. They have lots of money because they have no responsibilities, and they go around in sports cars." Lyle joined her—"That's right, and oh, boy, are they swingers! They don't get married because they have so much fun playing around!" I asked for proof of these sweeping generalizations and soon the group realized that both of these opposite fantasies were exaggerations. I asked them to think of people they knew and liked who happened to be single and they found that they were talking about themselves and others very much like them. Next I asked the group members if, in spite of being single again they were still the same acceptable people they were before the transition, even though they were treated differently by old friends. This question came up again and again before some of my clients could comfortably see themselves as singles.

Men counselors particularly may need to be reminded that this new social role can be more difficult for women than for men. Clients often discuss problems with dating, which presents a strange new world after years of married life. Young people can melt back into the never married group and begin dating almost as easily as before, and older men, in spite of new freedom for women, still have more social opportunities than older women. Men go out in the evening alone more freely than women, drop in at bars and dances, and get invited to parties more readily than women do. Of course some men are too depressed and discouraged after a divorce to ask for a date. Others feel shy and awkward approaching a woman. In our society it is still the man who is expected to take the initiative, and most men who are at least minimally assertive will eventually feel free to suggest a date to a woman who attracts them. In contrast, in my observation, it takes a very assertive or a very young woman to phone a man first and ask him to go out to dinner or a show with her. For a woman over thirty-five, brought up with the old code of propriety and modesty, such a move may be as repugnant as picking up a poisonous snake. Counselors may be able to dispute the irrational idea that rules about social invitations should be different for men and women. The women's movement has pioneered in this direction, but the revolution in dating has not yet arrived. Counselors who have worked with lonely and shy divorced men are aware that an unexpected invitation can be just as welcome and exhilarating to them as to a lonely woman, and can remind women clients that men and women are not very different in this respect. Thus counselors can steer women away from the old role of the coy, passive person who must sit and wait to be asked.

Women are much more likely to have women friends as a support group who can go together, for example, to a dance, which they would hesitate to do alone. While both boys and girls enjoy close same-sex friends during their school years, women are much more likely to continue to confide in their women friends after they are married. During and after dissolution, I find that women often seek others with similar experiences who can serve as sympathetic companions as they grope their way through their problems of adjusting to a new life. Whether from pride or from fear of closeness to another man, men do not seem to form these mutually supportive pairs or groups to relieve their loneliness, which, I am sure, is just as unpleasant for them as for their female counterparts.

Once dating has begun, counselors will find that new problems arise. Clients must cope with another role change, this time in their sexual situation. Marriage clearly defines one's sexual role as monogamous. After divorce the new choices may seem unsatisfying. Some women are shocked to find that the stereotype of divorcees as "fair game" now applies to them. Divorced at forty-five, Elena was a friendly person who was not afraid to travel and go to restaurants alone, but she was amazed and repelled by the number of men who propositioned her without so much as an introduction. When she stayed home she was even more shocked when husbands of acquaintances made similar suggestions, some even implying that they were magnanimously willing to "service" her.

Women and men who see themselves as unattractive and unwanted after a dissolution eagerly seek or accept lovers after a short acquaintance. If they are trying to prove that they are still desirable these sometimes desperate affairs will soon be less than gratifying. In *Creative Divorce* (1973), Mel Krantzler describes this as a very common phase following divorce, which ends when people find that a series of meaningless affairs is not satisfying. At this point, disillusioned but unwilling to settle for a life of abstinence, they may bring their dilemma into counseling. Here counselors can help them to redefine the problem in terms of self-esteem. Ruth, for example, was disgusted with herself after a series of short-lived affairs but found herself still seeking them. She explored what the affairs did for her and began to realize that they made her feel attractive and desirable at the time, but critical of herself soon after because she did not really care about any of her lovers. "I think I'm like an alcoholic," she said, "I want it at the time, but the next day I'm sorry, and then I do it again." I asked her if the affairs had really increased her feeling of being a beautiful, alluring woman. The answer was no—she felt ugly and miserable. Then I reframed the problem as a choice between feeling good about herself because she was an acceptable person or trying to feel good because somebody else found her desirable, not just a choice between having and not having sexual relations. Gradually Ruth began to see herself as an attractive person who did not need to continually sabotage herself with unhappy sexual affairs. Soon she was able to look for and enjoy some more satisfying friendly relationships with both men and women.

What happens when a person is not ready for a sexual relationship? Louis was very interested in Shirley but he was still recuperating from a difficult divorce and wanted to take things slowly. Like many other men, he feared that Shirley would lose interest if he did not become sexual early in the relationship. He did not realize that many women have the same fear of losing a new friend if they do not consent to having sex right away. I asked him how he could know what Shirley thought without asking her, and he realized he was making an unwarranted assumption. He wondered why he was so sure that Shirley would lose interest in him, when in fact she gave many signs of thoroughly enjoying his company. I continued to raise this same question until he could see that his fear of Shirley's rejection was mainly based on his own rejection of himself. In time he was able to see himself as a more acceptable person and could let go of his fear that Shirley would turn him down.

His next problem arose when he decided to have a frank discussion with Shirley but found he was afraid to talk about sex. I asked him "What would be the unfortunate consequences if you opened up the subject?" and he immediately thought of his ex-wife, who had refused to talk about their sexual relationship. The resulting confusion over their unclear nonverbal signals had played a large part in the demise of their marriage. Would he have the same problem with Shirley? Next he recalled his parents' absolute taboo against mention of sexual matters. I pointed out that Louis was still subscribing to old parental injunctions like a child fearful that his Critical Parent would punish him for saying naughty words. This helped Louis decide to let his Adult ego take over and approach the task in a problem solving way. At his next session he reported that talking with Shirley was easier than he had expected. As it turned out, Shirley had the same fear of rejection if she refused his advances. A counselor who encourages a client like Louis to discuss sex freely in the counseling sessions serves as a role model and provides an opportunity for desensitization of the too sensitive subject.

Jonathan enjoyed dating after his dissolution and was not yet interested in sexual intimacy with any of the women he knew. His problem was that he was afraid women would think he was homosexual. In a similar way, some women who are confused in their new sexual role after a divorce are afraid that men will think they are frigid until they prove themselves otherwise. Counselors can help clients face these fears and their reluctance to talk about them, and to learn that sharing their anxieties with a person of the opposite sex may not be as uncomfortable as living with their secret fears. For some recently separated people, years of unsatisfactory sexual relations in the marriage may prevent their beginning a new partnership. Or if fear of impotence, or of not having an orgasm is a problem, discussing it with a counselor may be all that is necessary to dispel the fear and encourage the person to level with a prospective partner. These clients may be surprised to find that a different person, a different environment, and different expectations may bring back sexual enjoyment that had been completely lost in an unhappy marriage.

This new, unclear sexual status may be so unacceptable to some that they avoid both the joyless abstinence role and the distasteful round of affairs by insisting on marriage early in a relationship. Fearing a shortage of men, many women have rushed into hasty remarriage expecting it to solve feelings of loneliness. If she has children and money is scarce, a woman may be tempted to overlook other important considerations and convince herself that she is marrying for the sake of her children. Similarly a man faced with the prospect of bringing up children alone may hastily seek a new wife as a substitute mother. Dependent and insecure men and women often remarry quickly, not realizing that they are really looking for a substitute father or mother for themselves. Unfortunately these people do not take the time to come to counseling before they marry and counselors are likely to see them when the new marriage falls apart. In a Seattle Parents Without Partners group several marriages took place shortly after dissolutions. Six weeks later, one partner or the other showed up at meetings, separated again.

A less frequent solution for those who do not find a heterosexual partner is to experiment with same-sex lovers. These people may seek help to relieve guilt about actions they never dreamed of during their married years. The same may be true of clients tormented with guilt about masturbation, believing parental or religious injunctions against such evils. The counselor can work on restructuring attitudes by asking the client to think through the consequences and list the harmful results of their sexual thoughts or actions. These can be weighed against the gratifications and clients can decide for themselves on the most reasonable course. I have found that some clients benefit from reading scientific, objective material about masturbation and homosexuality. The counselor's unperturbed discussion of these subjects may provide relief, as well as surprise, to those whose taboos have made them ashamed and secretive.

Other clients may feel guilty about any sexual activity despite today's wide social acceptance of sex outside of marriage. Objective discussion of the possible harm and the positive values, the old injunctions and the present fears, can reduce the burden of guilt feelings. Counselors can help clients explore the difference between sex that exploits or manipulates, sex that is merely a duty, and sex that is mutually satisfying. Many clients are unaware of these different meanings and the transition to a new sexual role after divorce can be a good time to clarify their desires and attitudes. Counselors who work with clients on these matters need to be aware of their own views and codes of behavior, and to withhold judgment.

Once a person decides to be sexually active, new problems may arise. A parent who wishes to have a lover spend the night may come for counseling, worried about how this will affect the children. In *Sex and the Single Parent* (1986), Mary Mattis discusses this situation. There are no rules of etiquette to follow. In one family the sleepy lover rose at four every morning and left the house to avoid the children. In another, the man rushed from the mother's bed to the living room couch just before the children woke up, an awkward masquerade that went on for years. The first step in counseling is to find out just how guilty the parent feels about the overnight lover. The real problem may not be the effect on the children but the parent's own conflict about the rightness or wrongness of the relationship. If the parent and the partner decide that the arrangement does no harm to them and in fact enhances their relationship, the more difficult step is to investigate the children's reactions. Children age four and under are apt to accept whatever parents do as natural. School-age children, on the other hand, may surprise their parents with their strict moral ideas as well as with the extent of their information and misinformation about sex. Adolescents may be the most difficult to deal with. Their reaction may be "If it's O.K. with you, then I can do it too." Parents who are afraid that their teenage children will follow their example may need help in placing boundaries between themselves and their offspring. Some parents find it difficult to tell their teenagers that adults have more privileges because they have more responsibilities, and to discuss the emotional damage that sex without responsibility can bring. Adolescents are notoriously good at arguing and blackmailing, and the key to dealing with them is self-confidence.

Counselors may need to spend a good deal of time helping parents see that they do have more experience and knowledge than their children, and since they are accountable for their offspring's welfare, setting limits is part of their job. For many parents this is difficult and they may need a good deal of encouragement before they can stick to their guns and enforce rules. If a parent continues to have trouble in these areas, family therapy is appropriate. The counselor can help the children explain what the mother's or father's behavior means to each child, and can encourage them to express their fears and their wishes. The counselor can model active, intent listening to children, so that parents can learn how to keep the lines of communication open at home. In family sessions, parents may be amazed to learn that their children are jealous of the intruder, or that they feel abandoned because of mother's new love interest. Boys and girls who have such feelings may hold in their anger, fearing further alienation or even punishment if they express their resentment. Counseling sessions can bring a variety of feelings to light, and give parents a good opportunity to understand and reassure their children. After everyone's thoughts and feelings have been aired and clarified parents can judge whether or not overnight partners or live ins will harm the children. If the mother or father is comfortable with the situation and can communicate that acceptance to the children, the consequences are not likely to be unfavorable. A series of different lovers will of course be more confusing and harder to explain than a more consistent, lasting relationship.

While learning to balance their new social roles, both men and women must also adjust to being a single head of household after years of shared responsibilities. While a man will usually have seen himself as head of his family, now unless his children live with him, he is head of nothing but himself. In his new role with no division of labor he not only must carry on his full time job, but perform many chores his wife formerly took charge of. He will be at a real disadvantage if his wife was a traditional homemaker and if he had never kept house for himself before he married. He must learn how to cook, clean, launder, mend, shop, run errands, and pay bills. This new role may conflict sharply with his standards of masculinity, adding confusion to his already diminished sense of power and authority. If his children live with him he will have to undertake serious parenting, which may have been a peripheral part of his life before. It is not surprising that a newly divorced man, feeling lost and resentful, often quickly finds a woman to share the daily tasks and restore his damaged masculine image.

Anxiety over his new roles may bring a man into counseling where he may begin to develop a broader view of masculinity. The counselor can help him see that gender roles are not absolutes. They are attitudes he has learned in society. A client named Albert was disturbed and resentful when he had to clean his new apartment. He saw this as a demeaning "frilly apron" activity and was ashamed when a friend dropped in as he was washing the kitchen floor. In counseling I helped him reframe housekeeping chores as survival skills that everyone needs to learn for comfortable living—skills he could respect rather than deprecate. As he learned to view gender roles less rigidly he began to accept some of the other stereotyped feminine qualities such as nurturing and expressing feelings as simply human.

Losing his status as head of the household and family authority was particularly hard on another client, Mark, who had a strong wish to control others. I asked him to explore the roots of this wish in order to open his eyes to its basis as a way of hiding his real feelings of insecurity. I asked him what would happen if he did not control other people and he exclaimed "That would be awful! They would take advantage of me!" We explored the source of this fear and found that he had been controlled by others and made to feel insignificant as he was growing up. He had to go to the opposite extreme to feel adequate in the present. Mark's intense fear of being an underdog is an example of the all-or-nothing thinking that keeps many clients from making reasonable solutions to their problems and keeps counselors busy pointing out the pitfalls of this mode of thought. As Mark became more aware of his unreasonable way of thinking he was able to see how his overly controlling manner contributed to the breakup of his marriage. In group therapy the members soon spotted Mark's dominating behavior, expressed their negative reactions to it, and contributed to the process of reassessment and change. Women as well as men can behave in dominating and self defeating ways.

When a woman finds herself the head of household, she too is likely to resent the load of duties formerly handled by her husband. Jean's situation is typical. She had never handled taxes, insurance, banking, house repairs, or car maintenance before. These tasks, in addition to her usual housework and caring for three children, were simply overwhelming. A more resourceful woman might have turned to the right people and asked the right questions to solve these new problems, but Jean was unassertive and did not like to ask for help. I had her role play asking questions at the bank and talking effectively to mechanics and other business people she had never had to stand up to before. When she found that she had to pay her own income tax, she panicked since she had no savings. After some role playing practice she was able to go to her bank to request a small loan. This accomplishment raised her confidence in her ability to tackle some of her other problems. When the frame of her screen door broke she did an adequate, if not professional, repair job. "And I had never hammered a nail in my life!" she crowed at her next counseling session. Clients like Jean may need a good deal of encouragement before they discover that they have more ability than they thought. Women are less likely to be upset at taking on some of the traditional masculine role activities than men are at doing womanly chores. Still, Jean described how awkward she felt at her son's Cub Scout awards ceremony when fathers were asked to come to the front with their sons for the presentation. The boy's divorced father did not come to the event, and Jean felt resentful and out of place among the men. "I couldn't let Danny go up there alone," she said, "but I felt so darn conspicuous."

Women who are overworked heads of households report that they receive less help and sympathy from friends and neighbors than divorced men. People are likely to come to the rescue of a newly single man with casseroles and dinner invitations more readily than to a divorced woman who can cook but may be just as lonely and harassed as her male counterpart. At one time in Washington, D.C., social agencies provided housekeeping help for single fathers but not for single mothers in the same economic situation.

Paradoxically, although bogged down with her head-of-family responsibilities, a divorcee may feel useless if her main role had been caring for her husband. Looking after her job, her house, and her children may fill her time but not her emotional void. The counselor can work toward improving the woman's self-image so she sees herself not as Cinderella but as a capable person as worth caring for as her husband. One client described her feeling of lost role vividly. After the dissolution Vivian said that grocery shopping depressed her. She could pick out the peanut butter and hamburger for the children but was near tears when she saw items on the shelves that her husband had liked and that she used to cook for him. At those moments her life seemed pointless and empty. I asked her why she was not buying the things she liked for herself. It had not occurred to her to give herself some treats to brighten her life. I had to work with her so she could see that being the head of a household consisting of herself and her two children was an acceptable and valuable role. She had taken a big step forward the day she told me that she had bought some oysters for herself. "My husband hated them so I never even thought of buying them before" she explained.

For some women the change to head of household means simultaneously taking on the breadwinner role. It would be rare for a man, with or without children to care for, to have to change his career as a result of divorce. But divorce forces many women into a less affluent, if not a poverty level lifestyle. As I have mentioned, support payments which are usually minimal tend to drop off after a few years, and payments are often late or missing entirely. There is no guarantee that fathers will not lose their jobs, acquire new families, move out of the area, or simply lose interest in supporting their children. In these cases, women may have great difficulty in retrieving the mandated support. Thus many women who have not worked outside the home must find a job right away. This desperate move is very different from thoughtfully planning and studying for a career and finding an appropriate and interesting position.

Even for a woman who has been working, her job may have merely supplemented the family income, or she may have worked part-time for a small salary. After divorce, if a full-time job becomes a necessity, she may be so dejected and resentful that she does not take a sensible approach to finding work. Forty-four-year-old Lucia had helped her husband in his business by working part-time at home as his bookkeeper. After he suddenly left her to marry a younger woman she knew that her transitional maintenance payments would stop in a few years. She knew that she would need a good job to live well and save for retirement, but her fiercely resentful attitude kept her from acting on this reality. In counseling she vented her rage at her husband's marriage, and at home she continued in her housewife role, taking on time-consuming jobs such as painting all the rooms, reupholstering furniture, and landscaping the yard. A timid woman, she was not only afraid of entering the business world, but considered having to do so demeaning. She found many excuses for not seeking work and not taking courses to prepare for a career. "He has plenty of money to buy a house for that woman! He can't make me go to work while she sits at home!" was her bitter complaint. So Lucia stayed home, as though this would somehow rectify the unfairness she would not tolerate.

A woman like Lucia is not ready for career counseling until her level of resentment is lowered. She needed help in seeing that she rather than her ex-husband was being unfair to Lucia. Until she could discard her unreasonable idea that things should be fair, she was defeating her own goal of having a good life. With Lucia, as with many clients, I asked for evidence that anything should be different from what it is. Next I taught her to say "it would be much better" if things were fair, or if the husband had not left, or if he gave her more money, for example. Until such clients can accept the tough reality that some things are unfair and cannot be changed, it is hard for them to take a reasonable problem solving approach. Before Lucia was ready to look for a job she needed treatment for her fearfulness. Using a desensitization procedure for taking small steps into the business world, I role played interviews with her, and encouraged her to find out facts about jobs where she could feel safe. She pictured secretarial and sales clerk jobs as the only possibilities. She began by looking up various job descriptions in the local library and found out about vocational programs offered by the community colleges. A vocational interest inventory suggested that occupations related to artistic interests would be congenial for her and so would occupations where she could work with people. Lucia needed a good deal of support and positive reinforcement as she looked for a job and as she began to work in a small dress shop. Gradually she gained some pride in her work and learned to accept her new role as a self-supporting woman.

If a single mother lives with her children, this new wage earner role will bring some practical hassles as well as a changed relationship with her children. Martha earned less than her ex-husband and had less time for the three young children than before. She described her struggle to make a living and her futile attempts to be both mother and father. Her day began with hurrying her youngest child to a daycare center and the other two to a neighbor's to wait for the school bus, and it seemed that she never stopped hurrying. She worried about lost wages when she took time off to go to court to collect missing support payments, and about losing her job if she had to leave early to take the children to doctor and dentist appointments. In the evening she had to do all the other necessary errands and chores that a family requires. All of this contributed to her short temper with the children. And when her ex-husband remarried, her grief and resentment, like Lucia's, flared up. Her three-year-old resented being away from home all day, and the school-age boy and girl resented spending afternoon hours with sitters or alone when the sitter did not show up. When they acted out in retaliation, Martha's problems were compounded. Tired at the end of the day and annoyed at their noncooperation, she was in no condition to give the comfort she knew the youngsters needed. Feeling guilty, like many single mothers, about her shortcomings, Martha sometimes went to the other extreme of indulging the children.

If a single parent takes time to go for counseling, the counselor can give support and encouragement to relieve the guilt that parents feel when they cannot be all things to their children. Counselors can help these people recognize that either they sought the dissolution because it was necessary or it was forced on them. In either case, no one was deliberately trying to hurt the children. Most single parents are working hard with no emotional support from a partner. The counselor can focus on what they are accomplishing by actually holding the family together and can provide positive strokes for their hard work and their wisdom in seeking help to improve the situation. This can increase the parents' confidence and nudge them out of the victimized attitude so that they can deal with their multiple problems more optimistically. I like to remind parents that they have the right to indulge themselves as well as their children.

In the midst of role shifts, parents and children may have to move to a less desirable dwelling. A father may find himself in a cramped apartment after years of enjoying a house and yard, and his children may have to share a room or sleep on a couch when they come to visit. Some mothers have moved into public housing for the first time in their lives or to low-rent projects where they do not feel at home. Both men and women can benefit from supportive counseling, practical advice, and a cognitive approach to help them separate their adequacy as a person from what they may see as shameful surroundings. I remind the client that he or she is the same person as before and I might ask "How can this little apartment change you into a less acceptable person or a less interesting friend?" or "How can this house make you a failure, when you are simply a person in a tough situation?"

Spurred on by determination to find better housing and improve their financial outlook, many women (but rarely men) go back to school to train for a career after a marital breakup. Some find becoming a student again is a difficult if not a frightening role change. But colleges and universities in recent years have enrolled tremendous numbers of women older than the eighteen- to twenty-two-year-old college students. Some of my clients have been apprehensive because they think they cannot learn as well in their thirties or forties as they had before. I tell them that knowledge and judgment increase with age and experience, and the chief decline is in perceptual-motor speed, which is hardly a requisite for academic work unless one plans to be a professional dancer or athlete. If a client sees herself as an object of ridicule among students twenty years younger, I ask her "Who has the problem?" Then I show her how to put the problem back where it belongs—in the youthful person who is probably revealing either insecurity or egotism. I ask if there is any evidence that age makes her inferior to her young classmates. Then I remind her that she has been successfully learning all kinds of practical skills, has probably read a good deal more, traveled more, and been exposed to many more life experiences than an adolescent could possibly have. If her classes are interesting and fit with her ability, she will no doubt recover from her fears and gain satisfaction in the stimulating student role.

Multiple role changes can cause a tremendous amount of stress. Dr. Thomas Holmes and his colleagues at the University of Washington have documented the great likelihood of physical illness for people who undergo several life changes in a short span of time. The Social Readjustment Rating Scale (see Holmes and Rahe 1967) lists death of a spouse as the most stressful transition, with divorce and marital separation being second and third. Other stress influences include change in financial status, change in living conditions, change in occupation, trouble with in-laws, and change in social activities, all of which may strike a person at once at the time of divorce. Thus physical illness may add to stress at a time when all one's energy is needed merely to cope with the transition. That so many people seem able to weather these blows without becoming ill or without resorting to counseling is surprising to me, but many months later counselors may see those who turned to drugs or alcohol or married hastily in response to the stress of divorce.

When clients do come in counselors can help them find healthy ways to manage stress. Some people benefit from relaxation techniques. I often recommend Jacobson's *You Must Relax* (1976), Benson's *The Relaxation Response* (1976), and various relaxation tapes. Such tapes may help worriers to fall asleep more easily. Jogging, meditation, or religion can be a great source of relief. Some clients may neglect their physical health in the midst of the turmoil and may need to be reminded of the basics of diet, rest, and sensible habits.

On the positive side, the upheaval and the impossibility of continuing in their previous roles may leave people open to examine their identities, personalities, and values. While counseling does not guarantee that anyone will find a more suitable partner, it can increase understanding of strengths and weaknesses so that the client can develop a satisfying new identity and find life rewarding with or without a partner. Aware of the many disturbing role changes, counselors will be able to help the newly divorced to focus on future possibilities and to accept the challenge of the new life roles.

6
Dealing with Depression

Depression probably brings more people into divorce counseling than any other symptom. Counselors need to understand the nature and causes of depression and methods to effectively relieve it. It is not surprising that people are depressed at the time of a dissolution. The end of any relationship is a loss that leaves an empty space in one's life. The emptiness at the end of a marriage will be greater the longer the relationship has lasted, and if one was unwillingly forced into the divorce, the loss will be even more traumatic. Sudden, unexpected break-ups create the most intense depression and confusion. On their wedding day a man and a woman have been chosen to be the most important person in their partner's life. The opposite experience—being unchosen—can be devastating. If the person also feels that no one else cares, the feelings of helplessness, loneliness, and vulnerability are a sure recipe for depression. Middle-aged people who place high value on youth and sexual attractiveness may think that life is over. One forty-two year old woman plunged into deep depression soon after her divorce when she looked at newspaper advertisements for gorgeous New Year's Eve celebration gowns. She told herself that she would never go to a dance again in her life and would never need another evening dress. Similarly, a miserable round of self-blaming can fuel a depression.

Even for those who wanted and initiated the dissolution, unforeseen consequences can trigger depressive thoughts. The unanticipated role changes described in chapter 5, may upset the belief that divorce was a good decision. Loneliness can be more oppressive than expected. Ambivalent feelings based on such thoughts as "I didn't realize the children would be so upset" or "I should have stuck it out" may bring a confused person into counseling. Each client will focus on a different set of ideas leading to depression. Some cling to the idea that marriages should be forever, no matter what. Some will not give up thinking about the wonderful retirement they had planned together. Others may decide that trying to enjoy anything without the partner is worthless, and some women are overwhelmed by the expectation of life-long poverty.

The first task of the therapist is to assess the seriousness of the depression, which may range from occasional bouts of feeling blue to the serious possibility of suicide. The Beck Depression Scale (see Beck et al. 1979) will not only give an index of the depth of the disorder but will give a valuable picture of what thoughts are most disturbing to the client. The Zung Self-Rating Depression Scale (Zung 1975), an abbreviated questionnaire, gives an approximate measure of the seriousness of the depression, with cut-off points indicating whether or not the person is more similar to those who need hospitalization or to those who can benefit from out-patient treatment. The Minnesota Multiphasic Personality Inventory measures depression and suicide potential, and reveals personality disorders such as hypochondria, poor impulse control, paranoid thinking, and psychosis. If a counselor has not been trained in interpreting these test scores, consultation with a clinical psychologist will be necessary.

Symptoms of depression may include not sleeping or sleeping too much; not eating or eating too much; having difficulty with job, housework, or childcare; refusing to leave the house or see friends; having tension; being irritable; and having poor concentration. Some depressed people turn to alcohol, tranquilizers, or drugs. If a client is deeply depressed, it is important to refer the person for a consultation. A psychologist who has worked with similar cases can assess the seriousness of the problem, and a psychiatrist well trained in the use of psychotropic drugs can evaluate the need for medication and prescribe an appropriate antidepressant drug. In some states a psychiatric nurse can prescribe medication. A physician will usually be needed if the client has to be hospitalized. Every counselor needs to have a working relationship with a qualified psychologist and psychiatrist. Counselors need to be aware that many antidepressant drugs take days or weeks to be effective, and the psychiatrist needs to see the client at intervals to monitor the strength and the effectiveness of the dosage. No counselor should continue to treat a person when the disorder goes beyond his or her expertise.

Sometimes I am asked whether divorce is harder for women than for men. While more women come into therapy for depression, men are more likely than women to suffer without seeking help and without expressing their feelings to anyone. I have seen men hospitalized after a divorce, unable to function without a devoted partner, and more men than women commit suicide over the loss of a love, as well as for other reasons. Women, however, make unsuccessful suicide attempts or gestures more often than men. A man may become depressed over the severed relationship with his children or may suffer from the loss of prestige and control. Women may have an advantage if they have kept up closer relationships with relatives and friends who can provide a support base. Living with children can be a joy, a burden, or both. Their absence can mean greater independence or greater loneliness. Thus the question of who is more likely to be depressed depends entirely on the individual's resources, supports, and ways of perceiving the situation.

Many clinicians have proposed explanations for depression and treatment methods that fit with their concepts. All may produce favorable results. Most, but not all, depressions eventually hit bottom and lift without any professional intervention at all. There may even be some advantage to a depressive reaction—its painfulness can drive the sufferer to re-evaluate his or her life or to seek counseling for the first time. The person may learn to cope with stress more appropriately than before.

Regardless of theory or technique, a counselor can be more helpful than friends and relatives the client may have burdened with complaints. As a model of reasonable objectivity, the counselor can inspire hope that the client also may some day achieve a more realistic outlook. The counselor's acceptance may be the first step in changing the client's idea that he or she is totally unlovable. The counselor can point out that everyone is likely to be depressed after a divorce and that other divorced people have recovered after a period of mourning.

After determining the seriousness of the depression, I recommend that counselors explore the client's sources of support. The recently separated or divorced person is likely to begin the first hour with a detailed description of negative events and thoughts, and a good deal of questioning may be necessary to find any positive features in the client's environment. Sources of support such as friends, church or club connections, enjoyable hobbies and amusements may all have been neglected in the turmoil of marital conflict and dissolution. A new client, Beverly, claimed she had no time for enjoyment. After working all week she had to spend the weekend doing housework. In the past she had found time to play bridge, sing in a church choir, and help neighbors with gardening problems, as well as doing housework and going to her job every day. When I pointed out that she had just as much time in her week now as she had had before, she was forced to agree. Then I asked her if her bridge friends, choir group, and neighbors were still available, and again she had to agree. Soon Beverly began to realize that insisting she had no time for enjoyment was irrational and not a good excuse for staying home and doing nothing.

Not only ideas, but feelings and behavior may all be dysfunctional in a depression, and improvement in any one of these areas will affect the others favorably. Some therapists see depression as occurring from an absence of positive reinforcement and have had good results by working to increase the number of pleasant events in the client's life. In *Control Your Depression* (1978), Lewinsohn, Munoz, and Zeiss suggest that depressed people keep track of daily pleasant events and notice when they elicit a better mood. They list hundreds of possible events ranging from picnics, dating, and skiing to taking a shower, listening to music, and daydreaming. One does not have to be a thorough-going behaviorist to encourage a client to list and engage in activities that once were enjoyable. At first clients like Beverly may insist that they do not enjoy anything anymore. Although Beverly was not ready to rejoin her choir or bridge club, she was able to appreciate simple pleasures like patting her dog (pets are often emotionally supportive), picking flowers, and thinking about a future visit from her sister. I asked her to keep a record of these positive experiences and assigned her homework of finding at least one per day the first week, then two a day the next week, and so on. She brought the record to each appointment and seeing the number grow was in itself rewarding. With other clients I have tailored the assignment to their particular choices, for example, to call one friend each day or to take a walk or a swim each day. Exercise alone can help to diminish depression.

I often set up a contract with a client to create an antidote for the depression. Some people are bogged down with unpleasant tasks such as eating alone, working at menial jobs, paying bills, or talking with the ex-spouse. After completing one of these unpleasant tasks, I tell my clients to give themselves a reward. Looking forward to a reward makes it easier to get through the difficult times. This method is particularly appropriate if procrastination is adding to the depressed outlook. The client does not get the reward until after the task is done. In this way positive reinforcement helps to get the difficult chores out of the way and allows for some balance in an otherwise unrewarding schedule.

As Beverly increased her pleasant events, she felt better and wanted to go back to her bridge club; however, the thought of returning made her tense. She worried that the other women would ask questions, that she would not be able to concentrate, and that she would be embarrassed by playing poorly. For Beverly, the next step was to learn some relaxation methods. I recommended Jacobson's *You Must Relax* (1976) and Benson's *The Relaxation Response* (1976). Relaxation tapes are also helpful. Anxiety like Beverly's often keeps depressed people from finding enjoyment.

Some clients sabotage themselves because they are afraid to initiate social activities or claim that they do not know what to say in social situations. Since social relationships are extremely important for depressed people, I help my clients develop more social assertiveness by recommending *Your Perfect Right* (Alberti and Emmons 1982) and *Assertion Training* (Cotter and Gruerra 1976). Many depressed people are not ready for the rigors of an assertiveness training class but can benefit from role playing with the counselor, rehearsing the social encounters they are likely to have. These activities can be combined with cognitive methods, which seek to identify and change the negative thoughts that cause the feelings of dejection. At the core of many depressions is low self-esteem. Many divorced people hold the opinion that their dissolution diminished their value as people. No wonder they are depressed! Dr. Aaron Beck, who has studied depression for many years, finds that people with low self-esteem are likely to feel "the four Ds"—Defeated, Defective, Deprived, and Deserted. This is especially true for those who think they have been treated unfairly. In *Feeling Good: The New Mood Therapy*

(1980), Dr. David Burns describes such people as acting as though they had REJECT stamped in large letters on their foreheads. (This book is in paperback and I often recommend it to my clients).

Howard sat in the back of the hall at a meeting, leaving early so he could avoid talking with anyone. For weeks Howard had avoided telling friends that his wife, Jane, had left. When they asked about her, he said that she was away, and he was vague about her whereabouts. He was so uncomfortable that he avoided friends as much as possible, which of course added to his misery. When I asked Howard to explore the thoughts going through his head he said "I'm thinking that if I saw my friends they would ask about Jane and try to pin me down as to where she was and what she was doing." I asked him to tell me the worst consequences if this happened. "Then I would have to tell them that we were separated and getting a divorce" he replied. I asked why this was such a dreaded event and he said "They will think I have done something wrong." "And if they do think that?" I prodded. He had to stop and think before he said "I guess they will think I'm no good." "And if they do?" I asked. To Howard, that meant that he was indeed a no-good person. The next step was to dispute the irrational belief that friends' thoughts could change him into a worthless person. I asked him for proof that this was so, and he could muster no proof. For Howard, whose self-confidence had been low even before the separation, his self-blaming thoughts were difficult to change. I continued to challenge them by inquiring "Does your adequacy as a human being depend on you or on what another person says or does?" and "How can a judge's decree change the nature of a person?" After expressing my amazement that anyone's words can change a person, I asked "Can *you* do it to anyone else? Can you actually change another human being into a worthless person by something that you say or do?" Gradually Howard let go of his unfounded beliefs.

Often I ask clients to check out their assumptions that friends will be critical. When I asked Howard "What would you do if one of your friends had recently been divorced?" his answer was "I would be sorry, and I would try to help out." This helped him realize that he was unfairly discounting his friends. When he finally faced them, they were sympathetic rather than accusing, and immediately began to include him in their social activities.

Sometimes, of course, friends do disapprove of dissolution. For some clients the critical attitude of even one friend may lead to feelings of being forever shunned and friendless. This unwarranted generalization is a good example of the all-or-nothing thinking so typical of people who have fallen into the depression trap. To them, there is no such thing as moderation. If things are not good, they are terrible; if there are no friends now, there never will be any; if I could not achieve a perfect marriage, I am a total failure. I try to dispute these opinions by pointing out the shades of gray between the extremes. Some day the lonely person will make new friends; things can be fairly good or moderately bad; marriages can have problems and people can make mistakes without being total failures.

Since the depressed client is usually the one who did not want the divorce, I may have to challenge the notion "I must have done something wrong or my spouse wouldn't have wanted to leave." Marily blamed herself for everything that went wrong in her marriage to Michael. Looking back, she decided that taking a job was a bad idea, and that she was at fault for not dieting and losing five pounds. Next she criticized herself for not always giving in to Mike's sudden plans for changing jobs, moving to a new house, taking an expensive trip, or leaving the children for lengthy stays at his mother's. Mike also made a sudden decision to take on a new wife, yet Marily still blamed herself even though she had cheerfully accepted most of Mike's unpredictable plans. I asked her if she was supposed to be perfect and to make no mistakes at all. I asked her if she had gotten up each morning looking for ways to spoil the marriage. Of course she said no and insisted that staying together had always been her aim. I pointed out that in spite of her good intentions things did not work out as she had hoped, and she was being as hard on herself as if she had deliberately destroyed her marriage. I reminded her that she was in fact treating herself more harshly than the law—the penalty for an unplanned murder is more lenient than that for a premeditated crime. She was also blaming herself for a situation that involved three people. Since Michael apparently did not want to improve his marriage or make changes in himself, Marily was finally able to see that she was not responsible for his behavior and could not make him change.

If a client continues to feel inferior, I may ask "Do you believe in democracy or fascism?" Most will say that of course they believe in democracy. Then I point out that Hitler condemned whole groups of people as inferior but in a democracy all are considered equal. Then I ask the clients if they really want to be like Hitler—after all, they are seeing themselves the way Hitler saw the people he classified as inferior. I am indebted to a colleague, Dr. Don Akutagawa, for this method of comparing self-critical thoughts to fascist beliefs.

If a client persists in the irrational belief that a divorced person is inferior or inadequate, I combat this by asking him or her to look at the difference between bad deeds and bad people. I ask the client to change the word *bad* to something less judgmental, like *unfortunate* or *thoughtless*. I suggest that all people make mistakes and commit foolish or even destructive acts that can injure a marriage, including the mistake of marrying too hastily in the first place. Then I help the client see that it makes no sense to confuse the action with the person. Everyone problaby does admirable things as well as heartless ones, so to label a person as bad is hardly accurate even though some of his or her actions may be unworthy.

This cognitive method is most effective if the clients first write down their negative thoughts, then follow with a more rational interpretation. For instance, if a client thinks "I have to be loved to be worthwhile" (there is even a popular song unfortunately entitled "You're Nobody Till Somebody Loves You"), writing it down emphasizes its foolishness. Then the client can write next to the first statement "I feel good when I am loved, but I am still an acceptable person without it." The idea that "Life is over because I'll never find anyone else to love" also contributes to depression. I dispute this by asking if the client is setting up shop as a fortune teller. A more reasonable counter might be "I haven't anyone now, but that doesn't mean I never will." Likewise "I can't stand being alone" can be disputed with "You are in fact standing it," and the client can write "I don't like being alone, but I am enduring it." If clients write their thoughts down, challenge each one, then bring the list to their next counseling session, they will take the task seriously and gain more than they would by merely talking about their depressive thoughts.

Albert Ellis, one of the founders of the cognitive method of therapy, emphasizes the role of demands—shoulds, oughts, and musts—in creating depressed feelings. Lucy's husband left her soon after celebrating their twenty-fifth wedding anniversary and their three children were still in school. Lucy considered herself a faithful, hard-working wife, and her constant complaint during her early counseling sessions was that Jim should have stayed, should have appreciated her, should have known that the children needed him. He had no right to leave. When I repeatedly asked for proof that he *should* have done anything differently from what he did, she continued to insist that he *ought* to have stayed. I pointed out that while Lucy very desperately wanted her husband to stay, that was not the same as believing he should. It was hard for Lucy to grasp that there was no real basis for the shoulds at all, and no way to prove that anyone should or should not leave a marriage. Because Lucy so strongly wished for Jim to return, she had converted her desire into a should. It took some time for her to see that her demand was nothing more than a strong wish and that her insistence that Jim should return was like a child demanding to have its own way. Certainly Jim had a right to leave, however unfortunate it seemed to Lucy, and she had a right to wish that things were different. As she learned to turn the should demands into wishes, her depressed feelings decreased. As "I shouldn't be rejected" gave way to "I don't like being rejected" her self-pity began to evaporate. She also learned to recognize her feelings and to understand them—tasks her demands had allowed her to avoid.

Many clients like Lucy insist that it is not fair for the partner to break up their marriage. But in fact, no rule or law mandates fairness in life. One has only to be aware of handicapped people, crime victims, or fatal accidents to realize that fairness is certainly not a fact of life. To *demand* fairness, especially in a divorce, is simply a daydream. I often suggest that my clients read *A New Guide to Rational Living* (Ellis and Harper 1977) and *A Guide to Per-*

sonal Happiness (Ellis and Becker 1982) to learn ways of disputing the unrealistic demands that contribute to depression.

While the cognitive approach can be a valuable antidepressant, I sometimes find transactional analysis equally helpful. I begin by helping clients become aware of the Parent, Adult, and Child ego states, and to distinguish between them. Lucy's shoulds expressed critical parental injunctions probably based on her own parents' demands. At the same time her unhappy Child ego state was insisting on having her own way. Depressed people are often caught up in the victim-rescuer-persecutor triangle. Victimized is a good umbrella term for the for Ds—Defeated, Deprived, Defective, and Deserted. As I explored with Lucy this helpless, passive victim role that made it easy for her to blame others and take little responsibility for herself, she soon decided that being a martyr was unattractive and not very smart. She took a giant step out of her depression.

Clients like Lucy may play Berne's games such as "Poor me!" or "If it weren't for him." Games like these and "Ain't it awful" are played from the hurt, helpless Child position. Clients who are ready to look at themselves and acknowledge their Child component can then decide to move ahead to a more Adult position of taking responsibility and looking for solutions to their problems. Like Lucy, who had to reduce the power of her critical Parent, Marily (the divorcee who blamed herself unmercifully for everything that went wrong in her marriage) was hearing old Parent voices saying "You shouldn't have let it happen," and "Why can't you learn to do anything right?" When she could see that these were Parent leftovers she could give some space to her Adult ego state, and finally could substitute some reasonable ideas—"I made some mistakes, but I did some good things, too" and "I did what I could to prevent the divorce, but I couldn't make Michael change."

I sometimes ask my clients who are learning to be aware of their ego states to write down their thoughts each day so they can see that "I can't manage alone," for example, comes from the Child state, whereas "I didn't get the job but today I'm going to apply for another one" shows that the reasonable Adult is in charge. Keeping these lists and working to increase the number of adult statements can be a challenge. Susan was a methodical person who enjoyed drawing daily bar graphs of her three kinds of thoughts. In time she increased the number of bars to accommodate a growing nurturing Parent part of herself with comments such as, "I'm going to relax in a Jacuzzi bath" and "I'll take time to play Frisbee with the kids." The latter is clearly an idea from her playful Child state, which certainly needs to be developed in depressed people. As Susan learned to nurture herself and let herself have some fun, her depression lifted.

In addition to diminishing the amount of time a person spends being critical like a strict parent or complaining like a whining child, the transactional analysis method can uncover the life script, the pattern for living that everyone learns in childhood. Alfred Adler, an underrated psychologist who long ago followed then broke away from Freud, emphasized the importance of what we learn in early childhood. One of his many contributions is the concept of the inferiority complex, which most of us develop as children because we are in fact smaller and in many ways inferior to adults (see *The Science of Living,* 1929). Sadly, many of us continue to cling to this inappropriate self-image as we mature. The life script is similar. Early in childhood each of us takes on a role in the family drama and casts the other members in complementary roles. A boy may cast himself as the weak, fearful one surrounded by powerful authorities, and may act out this role every time he applies for a job or asks for a date, whether or not the actual people fit the imposing roles he assigns them. Thus the script is acted out in every life situation. Suzanne, the only girl in a wealthy family, was waited on by servants and played the role of the charming little princess in her childhood and on through a romantic courtship. After she married Leonard, he settled into a relaxed husband role. He not only dropped his ardent courting, but refused to play the servant part that Suzanne's script demanded of him. After he walked out Suzanne was very depressed. It took many weeks of counseling sessions before she learned that the little princess role no longer fit the adult woman. It was hard for her to give up the old expectations and to learn to wait on herself. She complained many times before the new self-sufficient Suzanne emerged and began to give her some gratifications she had not enjoyed before. She even surprised herself by learning to be her own chauffeur.

Giving up the old script can itself cause a depression. Brandon had been thoroughly dependent on an overprotective mother for decisions and comfort. He married a woman who failed to fulfill this powerful mother role because she, too, expected the same kind of mothering from her husband. Two people, trying to lean on each other may soon make for collapse, and the marriage did not last. The divorce and resulting depression had in a sense been self-created, but Brandon did not discover this until counseling uncovered the life script he had unwittingly been trying to follow. Brandon's sadness continued for several months as he mourned not only the loss of his marriage but the loss of the comfortable little boy role.

One way to discover the early drama the client is trying to reenact is to ask for a favorite fairy tale or children's story, which usually gives good hints about the client's script. For example, the client who identifies with Cinderella may act out a "Poor me" drama, overworked and humiliated by relatives and friends. A person who chooses Jack the Giant-Killer may play a feisty chip-on-the-shoulder role. The first step toward changing is awareness, for how can anyone change a pattern without knowing what it is? One way to change the script can be as simple as providing a new character in the drama—a parent figure who accepts and affirms the client, neither criticizing nor infantilizing. If the counselor challenges helplessness or negativism and encourages responsible rather than childlike behavior, the client can gradually incorporate the new character and begin meeting the new growth-promoting expectations of the more nurturing parent figure.

Without necessarily unearthing and labeling the life script, I usually work toward relieving the depressed client's misery by exploring earlier life events and personality patterns. A client who has lost a parent in childhood through death or divorce may experience exaggerated depression when the new loss triggers feelings similar to those of the earlier loss, especially if the client was never able to complete mourning for the lost parent. Adults in the family may have been too unhappy themselves to help the children with their suffering, or may have tried to cheer them up by taking them to the circus or otherwise diverting them, rather than encouraging them to express their grief. An extreme case was Anne, whose mother died when she was ten. Her father put away all pictures and reminders of her mother and forbade the children even to mention her. When Anne was thirty-eight and separated from her husband, she came into counseling feeling very depressed. When she recalled those years of holding in her feelings, she burst into sobs for the first time. She continued to weep over the loss of both her husband and her mother, and as she was able to discard her mistaken belief that she must not grieve, she became less and less depressed. Modern counselors do well to follow the advice of perhaps the greatest psychologist of all, Shakespeare, who spoke through Macbeth—"Give sorrow words; the grief that does not speak knits up the o'erwrought heart and bids it break."

If the loss of a close relative or friend occurs in adolescence, the older child may be expected to behave like an adult, to hide grief and even take charge of the younger children in the crisis. Boys especially may feel that they must hide feelings and "tough it out." Not only past losses but a life-long pattern of dependency may trigger postdivorce depression. If depression occurs after separation from an abusive spouse, chances are that the person is reacting more to the frustration of dependency needs than to the loss of that particular person. Likewise a boy who was taught that he was incapable of managing on his own, or one who was so emotionally neglected that he learned to be very fearful of being alone, is likely to experience heavy depression as well as severe anxiety after the loss of a partner. Clark, whose parents both worked, remembered how he used to come home from school and stand at the window for hours waiting for them. This memory sparked an earlier one. As a preschooler he was enrolled in a daycare center, and one evening the teacher had to leave before the boy's mother called for him. Clark sat alone and terrified on the curb in the dark until his mother finally showed up after being delayed in traffic. Once he understood the power of these earlier traumas, Clark was able to see that he had more resources now for overcoming loneliness than he had in childhood. Seeing his old anxiety in a new perspective, he gradually reduced his terrible fear of being alone and became

more confident. Another lonely client, Jay, rushed into a second marriage where his dependency wishes could be met and his loneliness could be forgotten. Since Jay had not finished the job of facing and desensitizing his old fears, he continued to feel overwhelming anxiety whenever he thought his wife was being less than completely attentive. He did not return for counseling and his second marriage soon broke up.

Exploring the ways problems began in the past can help people who feel change is hopeless or who are frustrated because they cannot understand their own overreactions. Knowing that the old patterns were learned at a time when they made sense, and that new ways can likewise be learned, may be the first long step toward feeling better. The counselor can show clients that the old life script was adaptive in the past because it served to prevent or diminish anxiety. There is always a reward in everything we do, even if the reward consists only in avoiding negative consequences. Clinging to his mother was Clark's way of feeling safe. Family members are likely to reinforce childish feelings of helplessness and inferiority by overprotecting and feeling sorry for the child. Even being a mean kid had its payoff—people paid attention! Hiding unacceptable feelings saved a child from scoldings, and acting afraid avoided having to take risks. All children must depend on adults, but some get so much help that they continue to expect it from everyone; others receive so little that they keep seeking gratification from people. When clients see how their old ways of dealing with people made sense in the past, they can begin to recognize that circumstances have changed and that the old strategies simply cannot work as well as they once did. This opens the way for the client to decide on new and more satisfying behaviors.

After the worst of the depression has lifted, clients may still obsess constantly about the lost relationship. Joan spent a good part of every session reminiscing about her ex-husband and the good times they had, and venting her bewilderment at his decision to leave. Even while she was well on her way toward enjoying new activities, she would still burst into tears when she thought about their wonderful vacation in Venice, or about the horrible time when she found out that he had not gone to a convention but had spent the night with another woman. She brooded about what she could have done to keep him, or what she might do to bring him back—"If only I had gone fishing with him" or "If he could just see that I'm really more loving than that other woman." At the same time she knew that her husband had been a chronic liar, had neglected the children, and had given her virtually no affection for years.

Mixed feelings of love and hate may continue long after a dissolution because of our universal human propensity for attachment to another human being. None of us would have lived more than a few days in infancy without another person to care for our physical needs. Thus we are imprinted from the beginning with connections to another human being, and we never outgrow our need for attachment. Margaret Mahler (1979) and other students of human development have documented how infants move gradually away from their parents, then return to safe harbor after each trip. Growing children move further away and return less frequently as they play with friends and go to school. Adolescents go further afield, often ignoring parents in favor of peers, but returning for emotional and financial support in a confusing mixture of autonomy and dependence. Finding a marriage or sexual partner marks the loosening of the bond with parents and the forming of a new attachment. If a person has enjoyed dependable parents he or she will be more secure and less dependent on a partner for feelings of well-being than the person who lacked a safe harbor in early years. But any partnership that lasts more than a few months develops its own sense of attachment. Margaret Mead has pointed out that one value of marriage is that it keeps the pair under one roof while they work out ways to live together so that the new attachment has a chance to grow.

There is a clear difference between love and attachment. Love includes respect and admiration, attraction, altruistic feelings toward the loved person, and a desire to share time and space together. A marriage that begins with romance and is short on love can develop attachment over the years, but has a high risk of ending in dissolution. Battered women who return time after time to abusive husbands, and husbands who put up for years with hostile, unsatisfactory wives are clearly attached. In these marriages I can find little evidence of love although there is a good deal of dependency on the part of both husband and wife.

After a dissolution, the client who continues to obsess about the ex-spouse, now more hated than loved, may be compared to an addict. Kicking this habit may be more difficult than kicking a drug addiction since it cannot be done "cold turkey." Even if the former partner has moved miles away, thoughts about the marriage can recur often. In *Letting Go* (1978), Zev Wanderer, a clinical psychologist, and Tracy Cabot describe a twelve-week program for overcoming a broken heart. Some of their suggestions include putting away every reminder of the lost love, moving the furniture around, changing household decorations, and avoiding music that triggers the old associations.

For clients who obsess about former partners, Wanderer and Cabot recommend thought-stopping. When the nostalgic thoughts appear the person yells "Stop!" If in public the person simply imagines saying it. After a number of repetitions "Stop!" will automatically follow an unwanted thought. A loud bang, even shooting a cap pistol, is an alternative to "Stop!" Another drastic measure is to take a whiff of smelling salts or another foul-smelling substance, pairing it with the sad nostalgic thoughts. Even pinching oneself sharply or snapping a heavy rubber band on the wrist can eventually extinguish the thoughts. Wanderer and Cabot also suggest having a pleasant thought ready to turn to after the thought-stopping.

Writing down a "crime list" of all the ex-partner's disliked behavior works well too. When sad feelings start to return the client reads over this list of mean, selfish, or thoughtless actions, and may even begin to feel grateful for the loss. Another way to diminish old longings is to write a letter describing all the loving and all the angry thoughts about the former spouse, and to keep adding to and rereading the letter but never sending it. Since reading the letter over and over eventually becomes boring, writing out the obsessive thoughts may help to purge them. Wanderer and Cabot suggest that clients set aside about an hour each day to concentrate on their sadness, preferably in an uncomfortable place, such as sitting in a corner facing the wall. This helps to isolate grieving from the rest of the day and the painful position often speeds up the process of letting go.

I encourage my clients to reward themselves when they are able to go for a certain length of time without the old wishes intruding. I tell them to pick something they really enjoy—going to a show, buying a new plant, reading a good book, or calling a friend—after going for, say, half a day without the troublesome thoughts. Then I increase the time so that the person goes for longer intervals free from the old thoughts before enjoying the reward. By the time a string of days are free from the obsessive thoughts a reward will no longer be necessary.

To steer some of my women clients out of postdivorce depression I have to help them distinguish between the real man they have lost and the fantasy man who may never have existed. Phyllis described the unforgivable things her ex-husband Harry did. He refused to give her money, never told her where he was going or when he would return, kept a tight reign on her, and criticized her constantly. He was now living with the woman he had been seeing before their marriage ended and had no intention of going back to Phyllis. In almost the same breath she would describe Harry as she wished him to be—returning home as loving and caring as he had been many years ago. Often she talked of these two "Harrys" interchangeably, pouring out her tangled feelings and her confusion as she tried to merge these two into one person. I knew that the fantasy of Harry returning served to defend her against the pain of reality. While accepting her strong wish for things to be different, I helped Phyllis clarify the difference between the reality man and the fantasy man. The real Harry clearly no longer loved Phyllis and was determined to live with another woman whereas fantasy Harry was loving and begging for forgiveness. Phyllis finally accepted the fact that the fantasy Harry no longer existed. This helped her finish the process of grieving for her marriage. I have used this method with several women. Molly actually mourned the end of her fantasy man and almost seemed to be enacting a funeral ceremony as she laid him to rest. A man, of course, can be equally embroiled in a futile search for a fantasy woman who is never going to return. Even with physical distance and no children to keep the interaction stirred up, it may take years for some divorced people to give up the melancholy attachment to the former spouse.

While most of the depressed people I see after a dissolution are those who wanted to preserve the marriage, sometimes those who initiated the breakup also are depressed and come for counseling. They may feel more guilty and upset than they thought they would when they asked for the divorce. Darryl had been miserable for the six years he was married to Adele and was confused because he was not happy after the dissolution. He complained that Adele constantly criticized him to friends and relatives and harassed him with demands for more money, but rather than getting on with his new life and finding new interests Darryl was stuck in a whining victim role. The cognitive approach helped him look at the facts of the situation so that he would not have to buy into Adele's unfair criticisms. It was true that he had tried for a long time to improve the marriage and that Adele had refused to go to marriage counseling. It was also true that he had good reasons for leaving and that he had thought through his decision conscientiously, rather than casting Adele lightly aside as she insisted to her friends. This helped him to see that Adele was acting vindictively and he began to separate her problems from his. Whenever he complained about Adele's unjustified criticisms, I asked him "Who owns the problem?" This steered him away from his self-blaming behavior. At the same time I pointed out that he was acting out a helpless victim role. Without falling into the futile rescuer role myself, I showed him that, like all who are trapped in the vicious triangle, he was becoming the persecutor as he criticized and planned revenge on Adele. He was even letting his guilt lead him to do some rescue operations for her. The only escape from this triangle is the Adult ego state, which avoids all three unproductive roles.

As Darryl began to see his situation more realistically, he shed his victimized and guilty stance. Then I asked him to form a picture of his marriage if it had continued, and to vividly imagine the feelings of both partners. In his mental picture he saw the same old conflicts, the same old differences in values that made dissension inevitable and compromise impossible, the continual dissatisfaction and resentment, and the miserable feeling of being trapped. He saw his two children hurt by the conflicts, covering their ears or hiding in their rooms as they often had when he and Adele quarreled. He visualized Adele nagging him as before, and becoming more and more disparaging even though she had fought the divorce. In this unhappy picture he saw himself becoming interested in other women and easily tempted to find a more compatible partner. What he neglected to notice in this scenario was that Adele was also feeling trapped and that their marriage prevented her from finding a more loving husband. This last thought helped Darryl become more self-accepting. By the time he left counseling, he understood that he could not control Adele's behavior or her hurt feelings. And just as he could not control her, he realized that she could not control his feelings unless he chose to let her. Finally he was able to close the book on his marriage.

    I think there may be some value in appropriate guilt. At one point I asked Darryl to imagine the kind of person he would be if he had walked out of the six-year, two-child marriage without a twinge of conscience, and this helped him reduce his self-punishing reproaches. In any case, if people who have ended a marriage can accept a measure of guilt as an unplesant but common reaction, they may be less likely to waste time in self-critical, backward-looking thoughts as they begin to build their new lives. It is encouraging to people who are depressed after a dissolution to know that many have suffered through the same feelings and recovered. In most cases depression eventually lifts, with or without treatment, as behavior changes and thoughts begin to focus elsewhere. Nature is on the side of healing.

7
Dealing with Rage and Revenge

Not long ago a young man in a town near Seattle, enraged because his wife had left him, rented a bulldozer and demolished the family home. Later he assaulted the newsman who was photographing the wreckage. Within a week a number of angry men wrote letters to the vengeful young man and to the editor of the local newspaper applauding the man for taking revenge on his wife. Only later did a few people write in with sympathy for the wife and children who had lost their home and possessions. The unusual amount of support this man received is clear evidence of the intense feelings aroused when one partner decides to leave a marriage. Sometimes the legal process itself, with adversarial attorneys each trying to get the best deal for their clients, can escalate the hard feelings in what may have started out as a fairly friendly dissolution. Even in no-fault proceedings — which by definition are conflict-free — custody battles, visitation disagreements, and money issues may fuel anger that continues for months and even years.

While the bizarre bulldozing incident made headlines, thousands of angry people are battering their spouses, ex-spouses, and children, sometimes to death. Newspapers report almost daily incidents of violent murder commited by an estranged husband or wife. Often the estranged one, usually a man, does not act out his rage until his former mate has a new lover. Seeing this as an intolerable blow, he may kill the former mate, the new lover, and sometimes himself as well. Although it is too late to help these people, counselors can hope to prevent similar tragedies by preparing people to deal more appropriately with their anger.

First we need to educate our clients about anger. It is a state of arousal, often characterized by a hot feeling, and accompanied by changes in breathing and heart rate, increased flow of adrenaline, and tensing of muscles. These bodily reactions prepare us for fight or flight. Probably the human race would not have survived without these mechanisms that were so useful when people lived in caves and were stalked by wild animals. It is no wonder that we often feel a mixture of anxiety, fear, and excitement when we are angry. Along with the feeling of anger we have angry thoughts — "I hate him," "She's a bitch," or "You shut up!" Anger is different from the annoyance we feel when we cannot find our keys. Anger is usually directed toward another person and intends to hurt him or her. Faced with an angry client, it is important for counselors to realize that anger always has a source. Look for the hurt, the deprivation, the threat, the unfulfilled expectations, the humiliation, the helplessness that precedes and is entangled with the anger. Since divorce can precipitate all of these emotions, it is not surprising that divorcing clients are often too angry to think clearly about their problems.

In my work I have observed two kinds of people—those who are very much aware of and articulate about their anger, but often do not acknowledge their hurt or helpless feelings, and those who are fully aware of the pain, often to the point of crying about it, but are unaware of or unable to accept their anger about the situation. Men are more likely to fit the first category and women the second. Fighting is a typically masculine stance and weeping helplessly fits the feminine stereotype. Women do cry more easily than men in anger but are also as capable of screaming and throwing things as men are. Who doesn't know that "Hell hath no fury like a woman scorned"? Conversely, some men stoically control and rationalize their anger. Counseling both overexpressors and underexpressors has the same goal—to provide tools for handling the anger in more appropriate and constructive ways.

Although anger usually has negative connotations, it is important to remember that this powerful emotion not only helped us to survive in the jungle but still has some positive value today. Just as pain saves us from burning our fingers on a hot stove, anger signals us that something is amiss. It is also a great energizer, providing motivation for good deeds as well as harmful ones. I do not think that women would have won the right to vote if they had sat around drinking tea and talking about it. Their fury at the disenfranchisement gave them the necessary energy to fight, write, march, and lobby until they achieved their goal. Many battered women have stayed in the abused victim role until they finally became angry enough to leave. And those who began the move to provide shelters for the battered were often impelled by their indignation.

Anger can also give a person the feeling of power even though it may be illusory. One mother told me she had no wastebaskets in the house because she could not get her children to empty them. She could never get them to do anything until she got angry, then she felt powerful enough to get results. But the power was temporary—she still had to pick up the trash herself. One teenage girl who wanted to leave home told me "I think I'll go home and pick a fight with my mother. Then I can run away." I asked her why she could not leave without a fight since she wanted to go. "I can't just leave unless I'm really mad," she said. Incidentally, those traditional conflicts between adolescents and parents serve a purpose. Anger at their offspring helps the parents let go, and the teenagers' fury at their parents can help launch them into independence.

It is useful, then, to help clients channel angry energy appropriately. First we need to know how people feel about and express their anger. Because of its hostile intent, many may confuse the feelings with the hostile action. As children we are taught not to hit or hurt others, not to say angry words, and not to even feel angry. A child who is furious at his little brother and is punished for hitting may learn to feel guilty about the feeling as well as the action. Parents cannot always tolerate hostile words or looks. One mother made a big issue over the fact that her son gave her dirty looks when he had to wash the dishes. A father gave his little girl her allowance only after she did her chores "without comment." One woman client, enraged because her best friend had an affair with her husband, had such hateful thoughts toward her friend that she felt too guilty to appear in church! She was not guilty of any vengeful acts or words, but she behaved as though her angry thoughts could harm. Actually they could not hurt anyone but herself.

To deal with the heated conflicts that erupt before and after divorce, we need to know how people have learned to deal with their anger. As a child Ellen cowered in her room when her alcoholic parents fought, afraid that they would kill each other and leave her alone. Anger was so dangerous to her that she dared not risk antagonizing anybody. During her marriage she cried when she heard her husband talking crossly to the children. She fantasied about leaving him but she knew she never could. Finally her husband was so fed up with her tears and passivity that he left. Quentin was also a child of fighting parents, but rather than hiding he tried to break up the fights. When he got in the middle they screamed at him to "Stop yelling!" When Quentin grew up he did a good job of emulating their volatile, quarrelsome matter. Like Ellen, Sandra was afraid to disagree with her husband and withdrew from conflicts, but for different reasons. Her parents "never had a cross word." With this polite atmosphere Sandra grew up to be a quiet lady like her mother, unwilling to express anger.

While we obviously learn how to express or hide feelings, it is also true that we are born with different temperaments. As babies, some of us are much more active than others, and some of us react more quickly and intensely to all kinds of stimuli. These differences tend to persist, so that the famous statement, "We all boil at different boiling points," is based on a mixture of heredity and learning.

A study of Constance Ahrons (1981) shows that as long as three years after dissolution many people are still angry at their ex-partners. She found that only half of her group of ninety-eight men and women were able to have a cooperative postdivorce relationship. I found this easy to believe after attending a Parents Without Partners meeting where an attorney gave a lecture about the complexities of the state's laws on dissolution. At the end when she asked for questions, instead of inquiring about legal matters, one woman began explaining how the law had favored her husband and left her on the short end after her dissolution. This opened up a hornet's nest of similar outraged complaints as the members tried to outdo one another until the chairperson put an end to the clamor.

Understanding that the strength of the anger is proportional to the depressed and hurt feelings that caused it gives counselors a handle for reducing the resentment. The methods described in Chapter 6 for alleviating depression and restoring a sense of self-esteem and competency will also help to lower the level of anger. Focusing on the unhappy feelings rather than the rage may be a first step. The man who bulldozed his house probably had not had a chance to describe his grief and frustration to an understanding counselor who might have helped him move toward a more rational way of solving his problem. This man, like many others in the midst of a dissolution, was probably angering himself with shoulds.

A client who clings to the idea that things should be fair and no one has a right to leave a marriage may respond to the rational-emotive method described by Albert Ellis in *How to Live with and without Anger* (1977). Counselors can emphasize that things might be better if they were fair, but no law says human relations have to be fair. If a client insists "She had no right to leave me," we can ask for proof of this statement and can point out that people do have the right to change their lives, although others may not like the results. One might ask "Supposing you had suffered in a marriage to the point of no reward, would you have the right to leave?" If the client contends that the partner should have changed, I might ask for proof and say "Are you willing to change because your mate is blaming and nagging you?" Few reply "yes" to these methods that are often used in a futile attempt to save a marriage. If a client has done whatever is possible to prevent the dissolution, then he or she may give up the mirage and accept the fact that "no one ever promised you a rose garden."

Forty-nine-year-old Rodney was particularly insistent that his wife should "see the light" and come back to him. He insisted that divorce was unjust and he should have his way. After some particularly loud complaints, I asked quietly "How does this differ from being a spoiled child?" He paused, and this question was the beginning of a real change in his perception of himself and his attitude toward the breakup of his marriage. This blunt confrontation would not necessarily fit all clients. Asking which is in charge, the Child or the Adult ego state, would be a more tactful approach, and one I used with another client. Claire was so furious after her husband filed for dissolution that she clung to the irrational idea that a divorce was out of the question. "I just can't stand it!" was her persistent claim. I asked her to tell what she was doing in her new situation. She was going to her job every day, looking for a new apartment, and working out a budget. She had neither suffered a breakdown nor was she spending her days in bed. Gradually she could accept the fact that she could stand it because she was in fact standing it, even though she did not like the dissolution at all. Her reasonable Adult was in fact coping well with the situation.

Some clients say they are afraid of their anger because they think they cannot control it. One client vividly described her fear that if she started to say angry words she would not be able to stop. Others feel great power in their rage and do not want to give up anger, insisting it is an uncontrollable natural instinct. I might counter this rationalization by suggesting that sex is also a natural instinct and that we manage to regulate it. It is also true that cooperation is just as natural an instinct as aggression; families and communities as well as animals and insects can cooperate as well as fight. I advise those who claim they cannot control their rage to read *Changing Lives through Redecision Therapy* (1979). The authors, Bob and Mary Goulding, remind us that when adults say "can't," they usually mean "won't."

Often clients are disturbed by the intensity of the anger stirred up by divorce, and confused because they don't know what to do with it—"Should I just sit on it, or should I scream?" Screaming and pounding pillows for catharsis of anger have mixed results. For some people, such blasting off can provide relief or a chance to see the anger as foolish. For others, it may simply increase the intensity of the rage and keep the feelings stirred up. Popular articles and books have advocated getting it all out. Some writers give a long list of physical ailments such as ulcers, high blood pressure, indigestion, skin rash, insomnia, overeating, self starvation, constipation, and headaches that they maintain can result from holding in angry feelings. Suffering in silence over a long period of time with any intense emotion can have unfortunate physical effects. But clients need not confuse this situation with "biting one's tongue" out of courtesy in a social encounter. As Carol Tavris points out in *Anger: the Misunderstood Emotion* (1982), whether or not it is a good idea to "let it all hang out," depends entirely on the situation. Holding back is the better part of valor in dealing with a child's tantrum, an unreasonable boss, or a person who is likely to retaliate aggressively. The advice of counting to ten before speaking can certainly help a person calm down a bit and delay escalation of a conflict. The idea of chopping wood or scrubbing the kitchen floor when one is angry has value—it provides time to think about the best action to take and dissipates some of the adrenaline. Running serves the same purpose and incidentally can relieve anxiety and depression. Talking the anger over with a friend may put anger in a better perspective.

As for suppressing rage, disappointment, or fear over long periods of time, perhaps the worst outcome is that the person becomes tense so that it is very difficult to express positive or loving feelings with any spontaneity, or to have fun with other people. Over time this shutting down can certainly corrode a relationship. And often it is the person who "gunnysacks" all complaints who may explode later in a damaging way, like the wives who seem to meekly accept physical abuse for years and then suddenly kill their battering husbands. Thus there are no simple rules for expressing anger. Extremes of holding it all in or pouring it all out can both be harmful.

Although counselors will rarely see murderers or others who maliciously retaliate, many clients will be occupied with fierce thoughts of retaliation. To help these people, counselors need to think through their own attitudes about revenge. We are brought up with conflicting messages such as "an eye for an eye" versus "turn the other cheek." Our culture certainly favors punishment of children and criminals in spite of a great deal of evidence that positive reinforcement produces better behavior than punishment. It takes no scientific experiment to prove that vengeful acts usually lead to retaliation, so that the conflict escalates, whether between two people or two nations.

Counselors can use several methods for diminishing the power of the revenge fantasies that keep people from getting on with their lives after a divorce. Cognitive methods helped Marianne, whose husband left her after twenty-two years to marry his young secretary. Earl tried to be fair, leaving her their house, car, and a monthly income. Even though she had a good job and could afford private psychotherapy, she raged for weeks about her ex-husband's honeymoon. "He took that woman to Bermuda! I always wanted to go there and he never took me." She fantasized ways to sink their cruise ship, burn down their hotel, or have them attacked by sharks. With Marianne, I worked on reframing the situation in more reasonable terms. Using Albert Ellis's (1977) framework—A (the situation), B (the interpretation of it), and C (the resulting emotion), I helped Marianne see that it was not Earl's trip that was causing her misery; it was her perception of the trip as an act of malice toward her. When I asked her, "If you remarry, will you consider it appropriate to go on a wedding trip?" she had to admit that she would. When she could see that Earl's honeymoon did not actually deprive her of anything, her thoughts of revenge began to fade. She even decided that a trip with him would not be much fun anyway, and she began to think of ways to enjoy herself on her own. While she was preoccupied with her vengefulness, she had not thought about the possibility of planning a pleasant trip with a friend. After thinking through the futility of confronting her ex-husband with her anger, she finally gave up the idea and said, "I decided to keep my dignity."

Gregory, twenty-five, and married only four years, was less concerned with dignity than with getting even. He insisted that he would gain a good deal of personal satisfaction by burning down the house if his wife should win it in the settlement. He did not worry about the consequences—Gloria would prosecute, he could be imprisoned for arson, and it certainly would not produce the considerate behavior he wanted from her. Convinced that she had left him simply to hurt him, he felt justified in hurting her back. In counseling I asked him to make a list of other possible reasons Gloria might have for breaking up the marriage. With some help he decided that she could have been unhappy, that she could have had an emotional problem, that she did not have the strength to work on the marriage problems, or that she was following in the footsteps of her mother who had been divorced three times. It was harder for him to admit that some of his own habits had caused her to leave, but he was able to list the fact that he often lost his temper, that he spent hours working on his motorcycle when Gloria wanted his company, and that they quarreled when she wanted to spend time with her women friends. As he tried to put himself in Gloria's shoes, he had to acknowledge that he was not an entirely innocent party in the dissolution. His wish for revenge began to diminish after I helped him see that burning down the house would be letting Gloria control his actions and giving her a good deal of power over him, whereas finding a more rational solution would be acting in his own best interests. He grudgingly accepted the fact that taking revenge would put a mean Child ego state in charge, rather than a reasonable Adult. Children act on impulse rather than looking at the long-term consequences of their acts.

Some clients who insist that their divorcing partners are so villainous that they deserve retribution may respond to a different approach. Asking "Do you want to lower yourself to the level of this reprehensible person by behaving just as badly?" may cause them to have second thoughts about revenge. Others may be helped to realize that they are using up a good deal of time and energy in futile attempts to change the other person and continue the emotional entanglement—time and energy that might be spent planning good things for themselves. Actually taking revenge can lead to uncomfortable guilt feelings. Some people may decide they would rather enjoy the sense of power that comes from forgiving or not retaliating than endure the guilt. The goal is to help clients see that the best revenge is to give themselves a good life in spite of a shabby dissolution.

A simple method that I have found useful for clients consumed by anger is to suggest that they write a very mean letter, criticizing the former spouse in the nastiest possible terms, but they may not mail it! After this it is usually easier to sit down and write a reasonable letter, expressing appropriate wishes and requests. The first letter can even be an enjoyable way of defusing some of the irate feelings. Thought-stopping, which I recommended for dispelling sad nostalgic ideas, is another way of counteracting angry thoughts. Saying "Stop" every time the angry idea intrudes may be as effective as snapping a wide rubber band on the wrist or taking a whiff from a concoction of rotten eggs.

Even when clients have reduced their angry feelings, rage may be stirred up again when they have to deal directly with ex-husbands or ex-wives over matters of property, money, and children. For such clients it pays for counselors to have a number of methods to teach handling of these confrontations in ways that will achieve good results. Since most of us have been criticized and blamed, if not insulted in the past, it is easy to use these well-learned methods when we are angry. But like revenge, blaming and criticizing are more likely to escalate a conflict than to solve a problem. Certainly we need to stand up for our rights when we have been badly treated, but clients can learn the difference between defending one's own territory and attacking the other person's. Being assertive about one's rights is not the same as behaving in a hostile, aggressive manner, as Drs. Bakker and Bakker-Rabdau explain in *No Trespassing! Explorations in Human Territoriality* (1973). To stand up for our rights and ask for reasonable treatment is very different from verbally assaulting the other person.

How can counselors prepare people for hostile encounters? First, they can explore goals. Does the client want a satisfactory solution to the problem or does the client want to win an argument? Does the client simply want to hurt the former spouse? If winning and putting the other person down is more important that solving the problem, the counselor can point out that if one loses, both lose in the end. The loser, harboring resentment, will be uncooperative in the future, which will make things difficult for the so-called winner. Counselors can ask, "Why is winning important to you? What happens if you don't win?" The person is probably thinking in black-and-white terms. "If I'm not on top, I'm on the bottom." The person is not realizing that two people can give and take as equals, and can afford to lose a little and gain a little. As one psychologist has said, "Power is for people who need power." When I worked with Nell before a confrontation with Lewis, her separated husband, her goal was to settle some property matters equitably. She was afraid that when she expressed her ideas about the settlement, he would "burst into flames." She was familiar with his short temper. I began by asking for as many suggestions as she could think of that would help her achieve a positive outcome. First, she could pick a good time and place. A restaurant is a good setting, not only because people feel good after a meal but also because they act more restrained in public. Nell did not want to eat dinner with Lewis but a cup of coffee in a quiet restaurant was fine. (Alcohol is not recommended for embattled people.) We thought of ways to conduct the conversation. Going slowly, not interrupting, and allowing time to listen and think before speaking are good rules. To ask, rather than demand, and to be very clear and specific is good advice. Nell decided to take the list with her to keep on track.

More difficult was the question of what to do when Lewis disagreed and lost his temper as he often did. It would be hard not to lash back at him, but Nell decided to look at him and say nothing. This would give her time to think and time for him to simmer down. She planned to take some deep breaths at this point to help her relax. We went over the method of checking out her perception of what Lewis said, and asking him to do the same for her, to ensure that each understood what the other was trying to convey. As for arriving at a solution acceptable to both parties, Nell planned to remember that both she and Lewis were interested in feeling good about the settlement. She realized that she would have to make some concessions if she expected Lewis to do the same.

There is no guarantee that two antagonistic people can settle a dispute harmoniously. I gave Nell a few more ideas for dealing with Lewis's angry responses. I described the "critical sandwich," a way of conveying dislike in a nonthreatening way. First one makes a positive statement such as "I know you have good reasons for your opinion," followed by the critical statement, and then another positive like "I appreciate your listening to my side of it." At this point Nell suddenly exploded, "But why should I have to be so nice to him after the way he treated me? He deserves to be blamed!" She forgot that her goal was to have a reasonable outcome, and that being nice was for her benefit as well as his. Nell, like many clients, confused giving with giving in. Giving, in the sense of giving courtesy and consideration, is not capitulating. Giving is a way of taking charge and promoting cooperation. Still, it was hard for Nell to keep the focus on what she wanted rather than on blaming Lewis.

Since Nell was so fearful of Lewis's temper, I suggested a method developed by Dr. Albert Bernstein, a psychologist in Vancouver, Washington, who has taught telephone operators how to deal with angry customers who gave them a hard time. In a workshop I attended in 1985 he displayed a large picture of an ugly lizard. He described how he explained to the operators that when we are emotional our lower brain centers take over, rather than the cortex which is our thinking brain. He called the lower brain the lizard brain, since lizards are not noted for their cortex, and suggested that the telephone operators think of these irate callers as lizard brains. This was only one of his successful ideas that have helped these workers keep cool and that have been used by many other companies where Dr. Bernstein has presented his Angry Customers Training Program. Nell laughed as she pictured Lewis as a lizard and decided that this would help her to be more relaxed with him. Any method of injecting humor into a conflict can certainly help to relieve the tension. As a final exercise, we role played how Nell would express her viewpoint, and then she tried to play the role of Lewis in the confrontation. Anticipating what he might say not only helped prepare her for the meeting but moved her a little closer to understanding his point of view. For further help on resolving conflicts, I recommend *Getting to Yes: Negotiating Agreement without Giving In* by Fisher and Ury (1983).

I am indebted to another client, Holly, for a method of dealing with a critical antagonist. Holly's mother visited her frequently, continually criticizing her daughter's housekeeping, furniture, friends, and activities. Holly felt very put down by this until she devised a way to turn it into a game. She kept a paper and pencil handy but out of sight, with two columns labeled plus and minus. Whenever her mother paid her a compliment, she put a mark in the plus column, and for every criticism she put a mark in the minus column. The race between the two columns was uneven, and Holly chuckled to herself when the negatives won by a score of sixteen to five. This method worked well for a divorcee whose ex-husband had a habit of telephoning her to find fault with her handling of the children, the house, her money, and so forth. Keeping a pad and pencil by the telephone, she counted his remarks, and reframed the calls from an unwelcome burden to an interesting race. "I almost enjoy his calls now because it's always a shutout in favor of the negatives. And he doesn't know that he's doing it to himself!"

Some clients, who avoid direct expression of their resentments toward the former wife or husband, find indirect ways. One woman who did not want the dissolution got sick on two successive court dates so that the proceedings had to be postponed for several weeks. Would she have been sick if it had been a dinner date? Another angry client whose wife had ordered him to leave put off answering her letters and delayed giving her the financial information she needed for the dissolution. Falling behind in support payments, failing to have the children ready for a planned visit, or failure to return them home on time are covert weapons all too often employed. Trying to make the other person feel guilty is another resentment tactic I have observed. For example, the custodial mother sends the child to father in worn-out shoes or a raggedy t-shirt to convey the message that the support money is insufficient. In one case, a daughter's dress became a guilt weapon. The child's overworked mother sent a limp, faded dress along on a visit to the father. His new wife, highly critical of the first wife, sent back the dress neatly washed, starched, and ironed. If this maneuver was designed to induce guilt, it failed. The child's mother was able to laugh to herself, and thank the second wife for her work. The rewards of trying to make the other party feel guilty by playing "Poor me" games are meager.

Unfortunately, even with the best efforts at problem solving, some clients cannot come to agreement over the difficult issues that a dissolution can raise. The new profession of mediation has developed as a way of settling these disputes without the enormous expense of going to court. Often a mental health professional and an attorney form a mediation team either employed by the court or working privately. They listen to both parties, clarify the issues, and work toward a solution acceptable to both. Each person then shows the agreement to his or her attorney before signing it to make sure that all bases are covered. While several sessions may be required, and a compromise is not always achieved, still the process is a valuable step and is much less expensive than a court battle. Since both parties agree to the solution, it is often more satisfactory than a decision made by a judge. Some critics have raised the objection that an unassertive spouse can be cowed into submitting to the plans of a more dominant one. Certainly an alert mediator has to make sure that the less assertive person is really agreeing rather than just giving in. While mediation requires some of the same skills as counseling and psychotherapy, such as active listening, it is not the same. It is a complex skill that requires special training. I suggest that counselors interested in becoming mediators read one of the books on the subject such as *Structured Mediation in Divorce Settlement* by O.J. Coogler (1978) or *Divorce Mediation* by John Haynes (1981). Training programs are available, with emphasis on conflict resolution techniques and a thorough understanding of state laws that apply to dissolution. Mediators need to be knowledgeable in the areas of financial matters and taxes as well. Without this knowledge and training, amateur mediators cannot hope to succeed with an antagonistic couple. As mediation becomes more available nationwide, angry battles over custody, property, and visitation issues may begin to disappear from the courtroom. With or without mediation, counselors will still need to be prepared to help upset clients work through their angry feelings during this difficult transition time.

8
Problems with Children

Arnold Morris's face revealed his depression before he spoke. At forty-two, he looked fifteen years older. "I'm just stuck. I've known that our marriage was no good, known it since Betsy was a baby. She's the youngest. We have four. She's only seven, and I can't get a divorce until she's through school. I feel like I'm sentenced to ten years in prison! So what I need help on is how to keep on being a good father. I know how bad divorce is for children, and I just can't do that to my kids. But I feel so rotten I hate to get up in the morning." Arnold was involved in the first problem that divorcing parents are likely to bring to counseling. Sorting out the pros and cons of dissolving a marriage is certainly more difficult for parents than for childless couples. As we try to predict the impact of a particular dissolution on the family's children, knowledge of the psychological effects of divorce can be useful.

If a child has lived with abuse or violence, a sense of relief is likely to follow when the abusing parent leaves, and the child's behavior may improve. In virtually all other cases, children past infancy will feel a sense of loss and unhappiness when one parent leaves. Some withdraw and become morose; some become hostile and aggressive. I recommend that counselors read the important study by Wallerstein and Kelly, *Surviving the Breakup: How Parents and Children Cope with Divorce* (1980). These researchers found that five years after the dissolution, one-third of the children still had problems (none had needed treatment before), one-third were well adjusted, and one-third were in between. Most children who were doing well had parents who were able to communicate in an amicable or at least a nonhostile way. They could discuss the children in a reasonable manner. Another salient factor in the childrens' well-being was their frequent interaction with the noncustodial parent.

These facts give hints for counselors who work with parents in the midst of a dissolution. We can make predictions about the value of maintaining as peaceful a relationship as possible with the other spouse, and about the value of continuing contact for the children with the other parent, no matter how painful this may be to the custodial mother or father. The many studies of how children of different ages react to the trauma of family breakup can help to prepare parents for their childrens' behavior. Toddlers and preschool children who have formed strong attachments to both parents may feel abandoned. They may follow the remaining parent around, whining and clinging. Many children too young to understand the reasons for the divorce may blame themselves for the break-up—"If only I had been good, Daddy wouldn't have left." School-age children may show serious grief reactions and disruptive behavior or failing work in school. Some may be hostile to mother, blaming her for father's leaving. Adolescents have more friends and activities outside the home and can talk more objectively about the divorce, but they are good at hiding their feelings and may suffer more depression than they are willing to show. Some adolescents feel that they must be supportive to their parents who are under stress even though they too need more support than they are receiving. Recent studies have shown that college students are not immune to intense grief and confusion when parents separate, and even young adult offspring may be more upset than anyone realizes. Waiting until the children grow up will not prevent unhappy reactions. Counselors can prepare parents for the fact that many children keep wishing for reconciliation, even after remarriage has closed that door.

In counseling, Arnold Morris, who had been sure that he must stay in his unhappy marriage for ten more years, began to look ahead to the possibility of easing the transition for his children. He realized that he would still be their father and that he could plan to spend time with each of the four individually as well as together. He could talk to each one to prepare them and let them ask questions. His expression brightened as he thought about enjoyable activities he could plan, free from interference by his wife Celia, who always kept the children close to home. No more vetoes by her when he wanted to take the older boy and girl to a ball game! As he struggled with his decision, he looked more closely at the tense situation at home. He realized that the stressful atmosphere was making the children less spontaneous and cheerful than he wanted them to be. After divorce there would be no more quarreling in front of the children, no more hating to come home after work. Arnold finally decided that no solution was ideal but that the advantages of leaving the marriage outweighed the inevitable disadvantages. After he decided to end his marriage, he not only felt lighter but also looked more alive and energetic.

After parents have resolved on dissolution, the next problem they may bring to counselors is the question of custody. Arnold assumed that his wife would have custody, thinking that no other plan was possible unless she could be proven an unfit mother, which she was not. Arnold did not know that in the past, when divorce was rare, fathers were usually awarded custody since they already "owned" their children and had the income to support them. In the late nineteenth century, however, courts began to make decisions in the best interests of the child, which is not always easy to determine. By the turn of the century, mothers had achieved more status in the eyes of the courts especially when the children were young. They began to win custody as the primary parent. The growing knowledge of children's need for security, the stirrings of women's liberation, and the creation of federal Aid to Families with Dependent Children financial support in the 1930s contributed to the trend of maternal custody. In fact, up until about 1970 it was rare for a mother to lose custody unless criminal behavior, sexual behavior, or mental illness labeled her unfit. Arnold was surprised to learn that in recent years more and more fathers have been asking for and winning custody. Many men have begun to reject the stereotype that locked them into the breadwinner role and to take a more meaningful part in their children's upbringing.

Like these men, Arnold did not want to be a mere visitor to his children. He had heard of joint custody, but rejected it, thinking that the children would have to spend half their time in each home. I explained that joint custody means shared responsibility for the children's welfare, and that parents decide jointly on important matters such as health, education, and religion. The children may spend most of their time with one parent as in sole custody, or they may divide their time in various ways between the two homes. Families have worked out systems of having the children spend half of the week with each parent, or alternate weeks, or alternate ten days, or even alternate months or years. Some children adjust easily to these arrangements, glad to be with both mother and father. Some families cope well with the frequent chauffeuring and with the hazards of homework or favorite toys left at the other home. One advantage is that each parent gets a block of time off for rest and recreation that single parents desperately need. Another advantage is that child responsibilities are more equally divided. Studies have shown that couples with joint custody do not return to court with complaints as frequently as those with a sole custody plan. Best of all, shared custody takes the win-lose contest out of a dissolution, and children no longer need feel abandoned by one parent. Both parents can express their love through a closer, caring relationship.

For parents who are considering joint custody I recommend Isolina Ricci's *Mom's House, Dad's House: Making Shared Custody Work* (1980) and Melvin Roman and William Haddad's *The Disposable Parent* (1978). These books describe and advocate methods for achieving successful shared custody. Ricci stresses the importance of drawing up a careful plan for dividing the time, making the necessary contacts, arriving at decisions, and resolv ing conflicts, with the help of a neutral party, if necessary. She counsels couples to shed the love-hate relationship and to take on a businesslike partnership. She finds that even antagonistic couples, faced with the need for cooperating and coming to an agreement, can do it.

I was at first skeptical that discordant couples could manage joint custody, but what is the alternative? If one member of such a couple has sole custody, he or she can continue to wield unreasonable, hostile power, which may go far to explaining why visits and support payments usually slack off after a few years and why these people so often return to court. Because joint custody works well for many families, Arnold briefly considered it with Celia before their dissolution. However, he was moving to another section of town, and the logistics of getting the younger children to their elementary school were too difficult. Celia wished to keep the children with her in the family home, but the oldest boy wanted to live with his father. While there is no exact age at which a court will let a child's wish determine custody, Arnold Jr. was fifteen and rode his bike to the central high school, eliminating transportation problems. Celia accepted this, fearing that the boy's behavior, already giving her trouble, would only worsen if he had to stay with her unwillingly. Research has shown that boys are more likely to have problems after divorce than girls and that children are likely to do better when living with the same-sex parent, depending, of course, on many factors (see Hetherington, Cox and Cox, 1978). Arnold was delighted that his son wanted to live with him but was at first apprehensive about his ability to give enough time to the boy. He soon realized, however, that Celia would also be working full-time as well as keeping house. "I guess if she can do two jobs I can" he decided.

The Morris's arrangement, sometimes called *split custody,* is not usual since courts generally lean toward keeping brothers and sisters together. Each case is different though, so we cannot make firm generalizations about which kind of custody is best. Some fathers' groups hail joint custody as the best way of continuing to be real fathers rather than "Disneyland Daddies," whereas women's groups have pointed out that shared custody can be unfair financially. If sharing the child's time equally means that no support money need be paid, and if the mother's income is less than the father's, this is indeed inequitable. Critics say that moving the children back and forth is too confusing to them. Others stress the value to the children of a closer relationship with both parents. Case histories show that many children accept the back and forth life more easily than do their parents. In any case, joint custody has become a real option, and some states have begun to mandate it unless there are goods reasons against it. Ricci (1980) suggests that the word *custody* be dropped entirely and recommends that we speak of parents' rights and responsibilities instead. She would also drop the word *visitation* and say instead that the child lives in two homes. To emphasize the parents' new businesslike relationship, she would substitute *my child's father,* or *my child's mother* for the terms *ex-husband* or *ex-wife.*

Many couples fight ugly custody battles in court over their children where judges must decide on the best interests of the child. Some courts provide social workers to investigate these families before a decision is made. Sometimes the children have a separate attorney or a volunteer Guardian ad Litem to protect their interests in the conflict. I have often been asked by the King County Family Court in Seattle to evaluate couples, using psychological tests, to help determine their fitness as parents. In addition to standard personality tests I usually ask both parents and each child to make a Kinetic Family Drawing (1970). These are pictures of the family members in action that give hints about how they see one another. Parents and children may be interacting enjoyably or the family members may be in separate areas engaged in individual pursuits with their backs to one another.

If counselors can work with parents on making their own custody decision, they may avoid expensive, demeaning court battles. Seeing each parent separately and together, and seeing how the children interact with each parent, will throw a good deal of light on the difficult decision. Counselors need all the information they can possibly get if they are to be helpful in arriving at a good custody decision. Richard Gardner's *Family Evaluation in Child Custody Litigation* (1982) contains excellent suggestions for interviewing parents. He recommends asking each parent for facts about the child's early years, snapshots of the child, activities he or she enjoys with the child, the child's interests, and so forth. These questions are designed to throw light on which parent is more involved in the child's life.

Dr. Gardner also gives good suggestions for interviewing the children in these disputes. He begins with factual questions about the child's activities and about the family. Questions about who puts the children to bed or wakes them up in the morning and who reads to them or helps them with homework give information indirectly about their relationship with each parent. He might ask children to describe mother and father, and to tell about the reasons for the divorce. To avoid putting a child on the spot with a direct question about where he or she wishes to live, Gardner may ask "Where would your brother want to live?" followed by "Why?" Or he may ask "If the judge decided you should live with your father, what would you think about that?" Naturally most children love and want to be loyal to both parents. To be forced to choose may make them feel that they are hurting the other parent or that the rejected parent will be angry at them. They may even feel that one parent needs them more. All of these feelings are hard for a child to express to anyone. Counselors can be alert to the signs that a child has been brainwashed and is parroting parents' instructions. Other children may be quite open in their preference, sometimes for the wrong reasons. One child wanted to be with father because he had a color television, and another wanted to stay in the family home to be with her cat. In such cases one can ask "If the television (or the cat) were in the other home, then where would you want to live?" We can make clear to the child that the judge, not the counselor, will be the one to decide and that the counselor will try to help the judge. One six-year-old, who was sad about the separation and confused about the court hearing, said "I want the principal to decide." The older the child, the more weight one can give to his or her preference. Sometimes a judge will interview a child in private. Rarely will children have to testify in court.

If interviewing and counseling can prevent litigation, the child has a better chance of surviving the dissolution, free from the acrimonious struggle that court battles can escalate. In working with hostile parents we must be aware that their motives may be suspect. Some mothers are determined to keep the children away from father as revenge for his leaving. Some fathers are out to punish the mother and may make an all-out effort to win the contest. Either parent may try to seduce the child with promises of swimming pools, dancing lessons, or trips to Disney World. Some fathers think they will save money by raising the children rather than paying support, but are shocked later as the costs of shoes, dental work, and school lunches increase every year. One way to evaluate the parent's real interest in the child's welfare is to ask how much time the parent will allow the child to spend with the other parent. In some cases this willingness to let the child have a relationship with the other parent, in spite of all the anger, may be crucial in determining the child's best interests. An alert counselor may need to help less assertive parents stand up for their rights against threats or intimidation. Some mothers have settled for token support payments or none, frightened that the father could win custody unless she agreed. Both parents may need to be reminded that the child will be the loser if the parents cannot reach a reasonable agreement.

In addition to being aware of possible hidden motives in custody disputes, counselors need to know about their state laws and traditions bearing on dissolution settlements. Brenda, a thirty-year-old mother of two small girls, might still have her children if she had seen a knowledgable counselor or attorney before she left her husband. She had planned carefully to leave her eleven-year marriage, first finding a job so she could afford to move, then taking a small inexpensive apartment. She saved her money and hoped to be promoted to a better job so that she could move to a place large enough for the girls. She went back to the house every evening to read to them, tuck them into bed, and kiss them good night. For the time being it seemed best to leave them in the familiar home with their father, who she felt was a better father than husband. When she had saved enough money, she filed for divorce, thinking that as the mother who had cared for her daughters full-time for many years she would have no trouble winning custody. She found that custody can sometimes depend on the particular values and biases of the judge. In Brenda's case the judge was appalled that a mother would leave her children. He was influenced by the fact that her husband's attorney brought up an affair she had briefly had five years earlier. Not only were house and children awarded to the father, but Brenda had to contribute support from her slim earnings. I have talked with lawyers who advise that a divorcing parent will do better to stay in the family home. On the other hand, our changing mores and acceptance of living together without marriage means that living with a person of the opposite sex no longer brands a parent as unfit (which it often did in the past), and most states have adopted policies that limit fitness to actual parenting ability. West Virginia is the only state at present that settles custody conflicts in favor of the primary parent—the one who has spent the most time caring for the children. Since in most cases this is clearly the mother, court battles may be prevented, but disgruntled fathers may fight these decisions.

Before custody is settled parents need to talk with their children about divorce and listen to their questions. It is hard for many parents to explain the reasons for the dissolution without criticizing the other parent. Counselors can help by bringing the whole family in and helping the children express the feelings they may have been too afraid or too confused to reveal at home. I saw a family on the verge of separating to help them discuss the divorce as calmly as possible. The mother and father each told their ten-year-old son, Eddie, how unhappy they were together, how they disagreed on many things, and how they wanted very different lives. They had tried for a long time to accept each other's ways but explained to Eddie that they would be much happier living apart. Eddie cried and so did both parents as he begged them to stay together, and expressed fear that he would never see Daddy again. Both parents assured him that they loved him, that they would not divorce him, and that he would see and be with both of them often. They explained that they would not be able to get back together even though they realized how much Eddie wished for it. It was hard for Eddie to understand that his Dad could still love him when he planned to move away. Like other children, Eddie worried that if his Dad could stop loving his mother, he could also stop loving Eddie. Worse still, what was to prevent mother from leaving him too? Eddie had a hard time putting these ideas into words, but both parents reassured him as best they could. I reminded them that they would probably have to repeat their reassurances again and again before Eddie could feel more at ease. The parents did not explain, at this stage, that both were showing interest in new partners. One transition at a time was more than enough.

In a session without Eddie I reiterated to his parents the important reasons for avoiding critical or disparaging remarks about each other within earshot of their son. Boys and girls look up to and identify with both mother and father, so that parents become a real part of their children's feelings about themselves. To be proud of either parent helps a boy or girl to be proud of himself or herself. To be told that mother or father is no good can make children feel ashamed, not only of their parents, but of themselves. The child reasons that if father or mother is bad, how can I be any better? Counselors can teach parents to express their sadness, disappointment, and even anger about the dissolution without vilifying the other parent. A father might say, "It's hard on all of us that your mother had to leave—we're unhappy and disappointed. But she felt she had to do it, even though we can't understand her reasons. And I know she still loves you even though she isn't here" rather than "You bet we're angry at her—what kind of a mean mother would play such a dirty trick on her children?"

Sometimes I can help these angry parents by reminding them that the missing partner was once the most wonderful person in the world. Surely they would not have married a person without at least a few good points! This may help them remember the spouse's favorable qualities so that they can explain to the children that the missing parent, like all of us, has a mixture of good and bad traits. This can be a step toward restoring the children's self-esteem, and helping them accept the divorce.

After the dissolution is final and custody is settled, the next problem that clients may bring to counselors has to do with visits, or rather the time to be spent with each parent. Traditionally, courts have spelled out such plans as every other weekend, Wednesday evening dinner, half of Christmas and Easter vacations, and six weeks during the summer to be spent with the noncustodial parent. The length of the visits and their frequency may be much less with very young children, more as they get older. I have worked with mothers in tears or in a rage over a father who would not adhere to the schedule and always wanted to change it to suit his plans so that the mother would often have to cancel her own plans. Conversely, I have seen mothers furious because father rigidly insisted on his weekends even though the child had to give up an important birthday party or school activity. In other families the anger erupts because no definite arrangements have been made. Visits were to be at the convenience of the parents, and they never seemed to find a mutually convenient time.

Counselors can suggest that parents agree to allow some flexibility in their visiting schedule but with specific provisions to let the other parent know of changes ahead of time. The child, of course, is the one who suffers when parents cannot work out arrangements amicably. Saddest of all are the times when a child, dressed and ready, eagerly waits at the window for the mother or father who fails to show up. I have heard this scenario all too often and have recommended that the client be prepared for it, show sympathy for the child's sadness, and avoid criticizing the parent who may be irresponsible or may have had an unavoidable delay. Even if they are seething, parents can learn to say, "I'm really sorry Dad (or Mom) didn't come, and I know you're disappointed. But let's see what we can do instead. We have some time now to build that model that we didn't have time for all week." Of course the home parent will be even angrier if he or she also has to give up an excursion, but I counsel them to do their scolding of the errant parent away from the children. Again, the child's welfare must come first.

Even when the visits go well, children often return home cranky and uncooperative after the weekend. Teachers sometimes report that they can tell when a child has been visiting a noncustodial parent by the stubborn or withdrawn behavior on Monday morning. Sometimes it takes until the end of the week for a child to return to normal. Counselors can help parents realize that this almost universal reaction does not necessarily mean that the children were unhappy at father's, nor does it mean that they dislike returning to mother's. It may simply mean too many transitions in too short a time. Very likely the visits remind the child again that the family has separated and that the child can do nothing to change that. Sometimes a girl or boy has a wonderful weekend full of treats, excursions, and new toys so that coming home means getting back to reality. One young man whose parents had divorced when he was only six told me bitterly that it would have been better to have had no visits at all because it was so hard to come back from no discipline and nothing but fun at dad's to the routine, chores, and school at mother's. Many children feel tense while visiting the one who left because they are unable to show their real resentment toward the parent for leaving, fearing that they might lose the little attention they can have from that parent. Back home these pent-up feelings may burst out in irrelevant huffiness at mother, who decides that dad must have mistreated the children, or she may wonder what she has done wrong to deserve such behavior. The children are too confused to explain that nobody has abused them, that divorce is hard on children, and that it is safer to be angry at mother who stayed with them than at father who went away.

One mother reported that her young daughter cried and refused to get ready for the weekend visits with father. She concluded that the visits were bad for five-year-old Elaine and should be stopped. However, I learned from the father that once Elaine was out of the house and in his car, she was all smiles and had a happy time during the weekend until she had to go home. Then she put on a performance much like her scene when she had to leave mother's. What was going on here? Elaine was expressing some of her resentment at her back and forth situation, but more important, I think, she was trying to show her love and loyalty to each parent by clinging to each one. She was not pretending—she really did want to stay with both mother and father. Thus we can help clients explore the childrens' ambivalent feelings before parents jump to the conclusion that the pre- and post-visit hassles are a sign that the visits are not good for the child.

All too often father will try to "pump" the children about mother's activities or vice versa, not only putting the children on the spot but proving the parent has not yet achieved a complete separation. It is hard for a parent still half in love not to wonder what the former mate is doing. But to put children in the position of carrying tales back and forth burdens them unfairly and stirs up uncomfortable feelings of disloyalty if they have to become "tattlers."

Some parents, perhaps too angry to speak to each other, insist that the child carry messages about the next visit, or worst of all, about money matters. Counselors can help parents realize that using the children as go-betweens is likely to store up resentment that may later break out in aggressive or deceitful problem behavior, which will be hard for the parents to handle. And with such parents we can continue to work on the long climb out of the angry, entangled marital relationship to the more objective, practical association as co-parents.

What of the mother or father who leaves and never visits the children? Unfortunately a few people do not care enough about their children to keep in touch with them. Some will not settle for being a mere visitor rather than a full-time parent. Some are more concerned with establishing a new family than with retaining ties to the former group. I have talked to at least one father who loved his child but deliberately decided to cut off the relationship. It was simply too painful for him to be reminded of his former wife. While forcing a parent to see a child is not a good solution, making them aware of how much their children need them is important. I have worked with adult clients whose mothers or fathers left when they were children and who still feel the loss. One young woman could not conceal her anger when her father, who left home when she was seven, suddenly turned up for the first time when she was nineteen and expected her to be a loving daughter. "He was nothing but a stranger to me. I never wanted to see him again."

Another client said that he stopped his visits because it was simply too depressing to see his children and then say goodbye to them every time. In counseling he revealed that his mother had left when he was about seven and had never come back to see him. Three or four years later he saw her on a bus. They talked and she promised to visit him soon—she never came. The short visits with his children apparently triggered the old sorrow that he had never been able to express to anyone. Counselors working with a parent or a child who has suffered because a divorced mother or father has disappeared can help them be aware of the possible reasons for the absence. We can emphasize that the lack of visits is not a reflection on the child, nor on the parent who stayed, but rather a problem within the person who left. In any case, it is likely to affect the child's self-esteem far more than the absent parent realizes, and the child needs an opportunity to express his feelings about it and to be reassured.

An unfortunate variation on the theme of missed visits occurs when the custodial parent refuses to allow the other parent to see the children. In rare cases this may be entirely appropriate, for example, if there is danger of sexual abuse or any other mistreatment. Even so, the court may provide for supervised meetings because children have a habit of loving and wanting to be with all but the most grossly abusive mothers and fathers. If the court has mandated visits, then the custodial parent has no right to refuse them for any reason other than a serious matter affecting the child's welfare. Often I have heard fathers complain that mothers keep their children home for trivial reasons such as a little sore throat. While on the other side of the coin mothers have refused to let a child go with father because "he drives so fast," or "he'll take my daughter with him to be with those awful drinking buddies of his." Father suspects mother of deceitfully finding excuses; mother suspects father of lying about his plans, and mistrust escalates. Both may have the child's welfare at heart, but both are still in the vengeful mode of relating. If counselors get a chance to intervene, they can listen to the accusations and try to find out whether the child is really too sick to go or whether the visits would really harm the child. Or is this simply a way to hurt the other parent? We can ask, "What do you think it does to your children to have you fighting with each other and depriving them of a chance to see their father (or mother)?" We cannot remind parents too often that the best way to promote their children's well-being is to learn to talk reasonably to each other, no matter how much they dislike each other. And they need to stop trying to control the other parent's relationship with the children. Certainly it is difficult for a mother or father to stand by and say nothing when the other parent feeds the children junk food, lets them sit up too late, and forgets to give them their medicine. However, we can put these irritations in perspective and help parents see them as much less important for the children in the long run than a peaceful relationship between mother and father. Ricci (1980) stresses that each parent must allow the other complete control when the child is living in the other home. Her advice is just as valuable for sole custody parents as for those who share responsibility more equally. A good way to prevent or at least reduce these conflicts is to draw up a contract before the dissolution, anticipating as many disagreements as possible, and planning ways to settle them so that neither parent will be controlled by the other. Ricci's book gives many suggestions for such a contract.

One of the most destructive conflicts occurs when a mother refuses to let the child visit because father has not sent the support money. Father, angry at this maneuver, refuses to send the money until the child is allowed to see him, and the fight becomes a self-defeating stand-off. Often I remind clients that there is no legal connection between support payments and visits. Both are obligations, regardless of whether or not the other parent is delinquent in providing money or allowing visitations. We can remind angry parents that punishing the other parent also punishes the child. The child suffers if money is short; the child suffers when deprived of time with the noncustodial parent. Some fathers insist there is no point in sending support money since the ex-wife is spending it all on herself or on her boyfriend, yet it is obvious that the mother is paying for housing, food, and clothing for the child. If she is not caring properly for the child, the father can resort to an agency such as Children's Protective Services or can try to get custody rather than withholding money. As for collecting support payments, counselors can advise clients on the proper channels, including the use of new federal laws that allow for withholding payments from income tax refunds after all other methods are exhausted. Unfortunately, some resentful fathers circumvent this by planning to have no refunds.

Other fathers, at a disadvantage because child support can be legally enforced while visits with their children cannot, have formed fathers' rights organizations. Some of these groups advocate joint custody as a way of continuing to be real fathers. Others explore possibilities for achieving legal enforcement of their right to be with their children. If a child refuses to go to see the other parent, counselors can be helpful by first seeing the child alone. We may need to see a child several times before the real reasons for objecting to the visits become clear. A child may feel disloyal by revealing dad as the source of the trouble and may show more tact than many parents by refusing to criticize one parent to the other. The next step is to see the child with both parents, if possible, and to help the child explain why the visits are troublesome. One nine-year-old boy, Dan, was able to tell me and his mother that it was simply boring at dad's apartment. He was tired of looking at television but afraid to suggest anything else to his dad. I am amazed at how cautious young children can be during these visits. Seeing very little of the parent who left, they fear losing what little they have. Dan's mother was concerned rather than pleased that the boy did not wish to be with his father, but still too resentful to discuss the situation calmly with her ex-husband who had angrily blamed her for Dan's reluctance. When I asked Dan what he really liked to do, he told me of the fun he had playing outdoors with his friends, and getting away from grownups. I suggested that he could ask dad if he might take a friend along on the next visit, and Dan remembered that there was a basketball hoop in the park near dad's apartment. In the end Dan decided to take his basketball along the next Saturday and ask his father to throw baskets with him. Both enjoyed the change.

In working with noncustodial parents who want to improve relationships with their children, I extend understanding of their difficulty in trying to be a real parent on short weekends in a place not set up for children. I help them realize that they do not have to spend a lot of money on entertainment and treats. I encourage them simply to pay attention and listen to the children who may be just as uncomfortable as their father with the new situation. Taking a walk is one way of paying attention since there is nothing to do but talk to each other. I help these parents brainstorm other inexpensive ways to encourage communication such as cooking a meal together, reading aloud, or playing table games. Sometimes I advise a mother to disappear tactfully so that a father can see his children in the family home where they can show off toys and other treasures in familiar surroundings. While not all cases end as happily as Dan's, we can be guided by the fact that exploring everybody's feelings about visiting can usually uncover a solution.

Even when parents make every effort to avoid conflicts, children may still express their pulled apart feelings through behavior problems. Even babies may develop psychosomatic symptoms. One young mother, upset and miserable after her husband left her for another woman, reported that her six-month-old baby had serious digestive problems, very possibly responding to his mother's depressed mood that reduced her usual loving attention almost to the vanishing point. Children's feelings after a parent leaves are almost identical to those felt by adults after an unwanted dissolution. Feelings of abandonment, isolation, grief, depression, self-blame, anger, guilt, and distrust are difficult. How can one expect even a model child, confused by all these emotions, to behave normally?

When parents come in with concerns about their children's problems such as regressing to infantile behavior, withdrawing into daydreams, aggressive bullying, or school difficulties, I am aware that the parent needs as much help as the child. A parent who is distressed and disorganized by the dissolution, and preoccupied with survival problems, has little attention and warmth to give to a child. That they can muster the strength to bring the youngster in for counseling is a tribute to their stamina. I try to reduce the parent's anxiety by extending empathy and understanding for the difficult job of single parenting. Only after a parent feels comfortable with me and realizes that I am not blaming him or her for the children's problems do I begin to give advice. First we explore the extent to which the parent has been able to listen to the children's reactions to the dissolution and answer their questions. I encourage the parent to let the children talk about their sadness and to share grief with them. There is plenty to cry about, and the sooner the children express their sorrow, the sooner it will diminish. Holding in sorrow may produce an apathetic, depressed child. Parents can also encourage their children to put their anger into words and can assure them that it is all right to feel angry. Time alone with each child is the best investment a parent can make, even if it is brief. It is rare for a child to have the undivided attention of a parent who is not busy cooking, watching television, or telling the child to clean up his or her room. If overworked parents complain at this point that they do not have that much time, and if they begin to feel put upon rather than helped by counseling, I remind them that relieving the children's problems will eventually mean more time for themselves.

Having time or pleasures for themselves is hard for some guilt-ridden parents to accept as they try to make up for the loss of the other parent. No one can be both mother and father, and attempting this impossible task is a recipe for resentment. Some deprive themselves for the sake of their children, like the young divorcee who bought her own clothes at a secondhand shop and treated her five-year-old son to new clothes he soon would outgrow. She was surprised when I expressed some amazement at this role reversal. She thought she was just being a good mother. Some single parents go further, letting things slide into a completely child-centered home, with dinner at any time the children choose or even at different times for each child. Either from guilt or from following the line of least resistance, some single parents become martyrs to their children, trying to appease them by giving in to them. Children are rarely appeased, however, and usually become more demanding. They learn that although mother will become angry, she will finally give in if they badger her enough. The counselor's job is to help these parents strike a balance between their own needs and those of their children.

To achieve a balance in needs and to avoid the victim role, parents may need help on setting limits. Wanting the child's love and approval can get in the way of being an effective parent especially for people who have just lost their main source of affection and support. We can encourage wavering parents to send a screaming five-year-old to another room, to keep an eight-year-old in the house for a couple of days if she bullies her friends, or to deprive an adolescent of car privileges. These are difficult tasks even for parents whose lives have not been shattered. It is easier but usually futile to scold, threaten, and slap, and it is hard to find a punishment to fit the crime. Cutting off television privileges or grounding are often effective, but how can single parents away at work all day enforce these limitations? Punishments that cannot be enforced are useless and will undermine the child's respect for the parent. How can we help these beleaguered parents out of this dilemma? First, I remind them that the best way to achieve desirable behavior is through positive reinforcement. While mothers and fathers are very quick to give negative attention to their children's misdemeanors, they tend to ignore the youngsters when they are behaving acceptably. A harried parent will naturally heave a sigh of relief and forget the children when they are playing quietly together, washing the dishes, or coming home on time. Those are the very times when giving positive attention will pay off. When I suggest giving positive reinforcement or rewards for good behavior, some parents object. "Why should I reward them for just doing what they're supposed to do? That's bribery!" I explain that rewarding with candy, money, or trips to the movies is not necessary. Just the simple words "I appreciate" can be a real reward to a child who is tired of scoldings. Parents do appreciate it when things run smoothly and will find that putting it into words will reduce the occasions for punishment. At the same time we can follow our own advice and give positive reinforcement to the efforts these parents make.

Another suggestion for dealing with problem behavior is to encourage parents to help the child gain self-confidence. Aggressive behavior is often a reaction to the helplessness a child feels after a family breakup. In addition to showing appreciation, parents can find ways for their children to gain back a feeling of having some control over their lives. The best way is to feel competent in some kind of activity. Parents do not need to provide expensive dancing or tennis lessons, but can easily find tasks that a boy or girl can do well. A school-age child can learn to cook and take pride in the accomplishment. An older child might be given the responsibility of grocery shopping or adding up household expenses. Acknowledgment and a little praise for a job well done will turn it from a chore into a source of satisfaction and a step toward independence. At the same time the parent is relieved of some burdens.

Some mothers and fathers go too far in placing responsibility on children after a divorce, and use them as a substitute for the missing mate. A mother may call the oldest son the man of the house (at age seven!) or a father may use an eleven-year-old daughter as the chief housekeeper and babysitter. One mother antagonized her adolescent daughter by using her for a confidante and therapist. Another mother relied heavily on her twelve-year-old son as her escort and resented it when he went to a show with his friends instead of with her. We may need to remind clients that children are still children no matter how competent they seem, and the boundaries between the generations need to be respected.

In combating or preventing problem behavior, keeping in touch with as many relatives as possible can be a help, since being part of a group is important for the morale of both adults and children. Even if the parent resents the ex-partner, the children will need contact with grandparents, aunts, uncles, and cousins on that side. They are still the children's family, and can contribute to their feeling of identity and being wanted. Single parents need a back-up person when they cannot be in two places at once, especially if they lack relatives. These people would be similar to the Big Brothers and Big Sisters for children whose other parent is deceased or completely unavailable. One mother who had to go to an important meeting at the same time her daughter was in a baseball game suggested the back-up idea. Single parents could use such a person for children's doctor appointments, school entertainments, and those difficult times when a young child is sick but the parent must go to work. Retired people might enjoy filling in at times. Until such an arrangement is available, I encourage single parents to form babysitting pools and to help each other out as much as possible.

When no adults at all are available, children must come home to an empty house with no one to provide attention, guidance, appreciation, and modeling of acceptable behavior. Many of these *latch-key* children are on their own all summer as well as after school before mother or father returns home. Some are scared and lonely; many are resentful. One young man told me that as a child he was so angry at being left alone all afternoon that he wrote his name in lighter fluid on the kitchen floor and set it on fire. It is not surprising that some of these children become delinquent after a dissolution and that the parents are blamed. We can reassure parents that it is not their fault they have to work; it is not their fault they had to move to a neighborhood where other unsupervised children are getting into mischief if not outright delinquency; it is not their fault they cannot afford sitters and there are no supervised after-school activities in the neighborhood; it is not their fault there is a shortage of daycare centers. Fortunately some schools, recognizing the potential for problems in children of divorce, provide preventive group programs where the participants can share feelings, reduce isolation, and build competence (Francke, 1983). Jo Anne Pedro-Carroll and Emory Cowan (1985) have studied groups of elementary school children who learn problem-solving, communication, and anger control skills to cope with the challenges of their parents' divorces. The researchers found that the children improved in their behavior both at home and at school, and they became less anxious. Counselors could encourage local school districts to form similar groups.

While custodial parents may feel overwhelmed with jobs, housework, and child care, and may envy the childfree life of the other parent, noncustodial mothers and fathers may feel shortchanged and may come in with problems quite different from those of the residential parent. Often they feel grief at losing their children and guilt at having left them if they instigated the dissolution. We can help reduce guilt and restore self-esteem by going over the reasons for leaving the family. A parent who left unwillingly may feel angry and rootless, no longer an important figure in the household. He or she may feel the same unhappy emotions that the children are feeling and will need help facing the future in a problem-solving way. If the parent who has the children is downgrading the noncustodial parent, the latter's position will be even more difficult, especially if this has turned the children against the absent mother or father. If we can see these alienated children in counseling or if we can arrange family sessions we can let everyone air negative feelings, give explanations, and come to an understanding. If this is not possible, we can work with the noncustodial parents who may understandably be ready to give up on parenting. We can help them to see that their children still need their love in spite of all the antagonism. Eventually children will grow more mature and will be able to see their parents' problems in a more tolerant light, especially if the absent mother or father has the patience to keep trying. Even if it is impossible to see the children, I encourage the parent to telephone and write letters and cards to the children, and to send occasional souvenirs to let them know that he (it is usually the father) still cares. Many parents fail to realize how much these tokens can mean to a child and how important it is to keep in touch, no matter how negligent the children are about writing thank you notes.

In most divorces the father leaves the family. If a mother leaves, eyebrows are raised and questions are asked. Even if a mother sees her children often and contributes toward their support, she is likely to be stigmatized. Her own children may be more angry toward her than they would be toward their father for leaving. Without knowing all the circumstances, how can we make the judgment that it is worse for a mother to leave in a dissolution than for a father? A mother may come to counseling for help in living with or rising above critical attitudes. Counselors can be supportive and understanding, and can help the mother explain the situation to relatives and friends without apologizing. People do not usually advertise the reasons for separating so it is easy for others to misunderstand. In rare cases a mother may be deprived of custody because she was actually harmful to her children.

In an unfortunate situation, a vindictive husband, with the help of a clever lawyer, may have unfairly smeared the mother's character or her mental health in order to win custody, but other reasons are more likely. She and her husband might have decided together that it would be more practical for father to keep the house and the children. I worked with Joanne, a busy professional woman, who left her five-year-old boy, Zach, with his father while she took on a new, demanding job and moved into a city apartment. She was sure that her boy would be better off with his father who worked at home more than half the time and had a very good relationship with his son. Zach would be with his usual friends and sitters and in his familiar kindergarten. Joanne knew that her new location was unsuitable for children and that the transition would be traumatic for him. She realized that Zach missed her and was upset, but she knew that if she took him with her, he would be just as unhappy at losing his dad. She needed help on dealing with her mother who criticized her unmercifully. In counseling I helped her put the problem back in perspective as belonging to her mother, whose rigid ideas of a mother's role were not going to change. I encouraged her to avoid arguing, which only gave the mother more ammunition. Joanne learned to listen, to say "I'm really sorry you feel that way," and to change the subject as quickly as possible. It makes no sense to characterize noncustodial mothers as lacking in maternal interest. Some are too emotionally overwhelmed by the divorce to cope with the children, and some think that the fathers are better at parenting. In one case a father kept the children out of consideration for his ex-wife, who was having a difficult time on a new job and needed a break. Sometimes the child's needs lead to the unusual custody decision. It makes sense for a boisterous, athletic boy to live with an outdoor-type father, and the mother may be relieved that she does not have to deal with her son and his football team friends. In any case, it is important for a mother to explain her reasons for leaving and reassure the children by her actions as well as her words that she still loves them.

No matter how much conflict has occurred in settling custody, most parents have to learn to live with the final decision even if they dislike it. But sometimes disputes escalate into a serious crime. A parent, with or without custody, takes the children and moves away. The horrible uncertainty about where the children are and how they are being cared for is as difficult to live with as the loss. We can provide supportive counseling to parents whose children have been kidnapped, can encourage them to seek legal help, and can recommend organizations that look for missing children. Many of the children whose photographs appear on television and on milk cartons have been kidnapped by their own parents, sometimes with the good intent of rescuing them from harmful situations, and sometimes out of sheer vengeance. If we have an opportunity to work with a would-be child snatcher, we can counsel him or her to be aware of the tragic consequences to a child of losing a mother or father abruptly and forever. We are hardly likely to see a vindictive kidnapper, but if a parent is contemplating such a move to rescue a child from a bad situation, counseling may prevent the crime. We can warn about behavior problems if a child is cut off from either parent, grandparents, and other familiar people, and we can give advice about legal remedies. Counseling may help the unhappy parent accept the fact that the children will have to stay where they are, and we can point out that keeping up a good relationship with them will go far toward diluting the effects of whatever unfavorable influences they live with.

It is not surprising that more books have been written about treating children than about treating adults in a dissolution. Excellent help for counselors who see children is available in Dr. Richard Gardner's *Psychotherapy with Children of Divorce* (1976) and Dr. Lora Tessman's comprehensive *Children of Parting Parents* (1978). Dr. Gardner has written a helpful book for children, *The Boys and Girls Book about Divorce* (1970). Many people who have lived through divorce have written books to guide parents and children through the hazards. Some of these are listed in the bibliography.

In spite of all the books, and in spite of the best efforts of counselors and of single parents themselves, too many children are living in poverty, lonely and unattended after school. The United States is almost alone among industrialized countries in not providing medical care, child allowances, and public daycare centers, all of which would greatly benefit the children of divorce. Until we recognize that we have a national problem, these children will continue to be the victims of the divorces they never planned or wanted.

9
Counseling for Postdivorce Adjustment and Growth

After they have divided up their property and decided on how to share their children, and after the emotional healing has begun, divorced people can give more attention to the question of "Where do I go from here?" Many writers describe the process of divorce as proceeding in definite stages, like the stages of accepting death and bereavement. These usually include shock, denial, grief, anger, mourning, and finally acceptance. Joy and David Rice give a thorough discussion of the various stage theories in *Living through Divorce: A Developmental Approach to Divorce Therapy* (1986). I find, however, that these states of mind do not progress in an orderly way. They may alternate unpredictably or several may torment a person at the same time. Even after acceptance, a reminder of the past may bring back sadness or anger, or a new turn of events may produce another shock. Robert Weiss, author of *Marital Separation* (1975), has studied hundreds of people in his Seminars for the Separated, and finds that it takes from two to four years for most people to recover from the trauma of divorce and accept the loss, however reluctantly. Since this transition happens gradually, many continue in counseling for a long time after their dissolution.

As they work on their plans for the future these clients still need the counselor's warmth and empathy as well as objectivity. They still need to be reminded that they are not alone, that others have been through what they are experiencing, and that others have survived. The old way of life is gone, yet now there is the possibility of making a new kind of life with different but satisfying options. One forty-year-old woman found solace after her husband left by reading Emerson's "Essay on Compensation" (1890). She could not quote the exact words, but the message was "Every time one door closes, another one opens, one you never could have explored if you had stayed in the same old place." Emerson points out that even a tragic loss can lead to growth in new directions. His other message that "The thief steals only from himself" also applies and is similar to the rational-emotive view that we are responsible for hurting or helping ourselves. If we hang on to blaming and self-pity after a dissolution, rather than finding ways to rebuild our lives, we are damaging only ourselves.

As counselors work with clients on the quest for tools to make good lives, they need to remember that in the passage through divorce no two clients are alike. Working on people on postdivorce adjustment calls for a wide variety of approaches. As Nancy Schlossberg points out in *Counseling Adults in Transition* (1984), reaching goals after a major change such as divorce depends on several factors—the person's own stage of development and coping resources, the immediate social supports, and the socioeconomic status and environment. As Erik Erikson emphasizes in *Childhood and Society* (1963), adults develop in their capacity to form intimate relationships and to make vocational choices. They can grow more altruistic and better able to make independent decisions, and more comfortable with accepting things they cannot change. There is no timetable that sets a particular age when these changes will take place, if in fact they do. Because we all acquire new interests and values as we grow, middle-aged and older people will be very different from one another.

Differences in the social surroundings of each client will suggest different approaches for counselors. Some newly single people can be encouraged to turn to family members, a social network, church groups, and work connections. By contrast, I have worked with several women who married American servicemen in Japan or Germany, came to this country speaking little English, had children, and were divorced before they were able to establish any real ties outside their homes. A large city or university town may offer extension classes, Displaced Homemaker programs, clubs, and good libraries and bookstores. When working with people from isolated communities, or with segregated ethnic groups, counselors may have to depend more on their own and their clients' ingenuity to find or create helpful postdivorce activities.

Most people want to find satisfaction in personal relations, in some kind of work, and in leisure activities and fun. Of course, these areas are not of equal importance to all clients. Some will be preoccupied with the search for a new intimate relationship, others with finding a satisfying kind of work. For another client, perhaps a senior citizen, finding leisure activities to replace those of married life may be the most important. One retired worker, Sidney Freidberg, combines his search for friendships with pursuit of leisure by inviting different women for lunch, concerts, parties, and lectures. In an article "On the Town with the Senior Single" in *Modern Maturity* (April-May 1986) Freidberg mentions that some women he has met are not afraid to take the initiative in suggesting a date. However, many woman are not as liberated, and men counselors may not realize that the search for a new partner is much more difficult for a woman than for a man. Or a woman counselor who values personal relationships as more crucial than an interesting job may not understand a man who seems satisfied burying himself in his work after divorce rather than seeking a social life.

Since we do not pick our clients to match ourselves in age, we need to be aware of the impact of divorce at different stages in life. Young counselors who see the need for intimacy with a partner as salient may not realize how a sixty-year-old person can satisfy this need by enjoying friends and grandchildren. A fifty-year-old man might be more likely to feel sure of his identity and his ability than a twenty-nine-year-old still floundering to find himself. Older adults, having weathered crises and transitions, may have developed good coping skills, but on the other hand, a dissolution after a thirty-year marriage can be much more disruptive than one that occurs after a brief one.

In addition to examining our own attitudes toward the age, gender, and social environments of our clients, we need to be aware of our feelings about being single, so that we can model an optimistic outlook on life after divorce. Fortunately the public perception of singleness is changing, perhaps because of the sheer numbers of unmarried people, and this lessening prejudice will certainly make the transition easier.

As we work toward increasing our clients' feelings that they are acceptable people who can live with confidence and autonomy, all the previous work in reducing the depressed, angry, and guilty thoughts surrounding the dissolution will have improved their self-image. The next step might be to take an inventory of assets. Making a list of abilities and accomplishments may help a person view himself (herself) in a positive light. Most clients have shown themselves capable of completing some education, holding a job, and making friends. Many have managed a household, cared for babies, and guided older children, all of which take emotional and physical stamina. Some clients overlook volunteer activities as unimportant, when in fact chairing a committee or teaching a Sunday school class demonstrates leadership ability. Listing these assets may help a client give up the old idea that "I'm a failure because I couldn't keep my marriage together." Single parents can be reminded that they have kept the remaining family functioning without the help of a partner, not an easy task.

Although psychological evaluations are expensive and may be out of the question financially for many clients, I recommend having a clinical psychologist give and interpret the results of psychological tests in those cases where the counselor wants an objective evaluation of a client's emotional resources. If the client is too scattered, or rigid, or lacking the strength to make decisions, a referral to a therapist equipped to give intensive psychotherapy or possibly to hospitalize the client may be necessary. Even responsible, well-functioning people may temporarily break down after a dissolution.

For those who are ready to move on to a new life, finding a new partner is often the main goal. In a recent study of midlife divorce, Elizabeth Cauhape found that a minority in her group were glad to be single again and did not intend to remarry but most of her subjects did seek a new partner. Her book, *Fresh Starts: Men and Women after Divorce* (1983), like several other books on the subject, describes those who go about the search in a frantic hurry. Other people take their time, look around and keep their options open. Methods vary widely. Some concentrate their search in their existing social networks; others set out to sample all kinds of new experiences.

Counselors may have a hard time understanding those who make a career of singles bars and one-night stands or who have confidence in computer matching services and magazine advertisements by people who wish to meet members of the opposite sex. To put these methods in perspective, we can remember that it is difficult for unattached people to find friends in our mobile urban society, where we have moved away from our families and cannot always find congenial neighbors next door. Perhaps dating services and personal advertisements serve the same function as the old-fashioned matchmaker. Jean Bryant, in her booklet *Playing the Personals* (1983), suggests that placing an advertisement in the spirit of play rather than in hopes of finding a dream mate can be a way to widen social contacts. Usually the replies to the advertisement go to a mailbox so you can remain anonymous. Sorting out the replies and deciding which people to telephone can be fun. After talking with a person, you can decide whether or not to meet and get acquainted. Bryant points out that if you describe yourself and your expectations accurately, and specify the kind of person you want to meet, the method may be a real shortcut to finding a congenial friend. Some national magazines have advertisements for networks of single people interested in books, art, or music, offering opportunities for finding friends with similar interests.

These methods may be more appropriate than singles bars and parties, which bring together a mix of people whose only common denominator is their single status. One client tried some singles' parties and found no one with congenial interests or similar background. Tired of this approach, she concluded that she was like the man who was searching under a lamp post for his lost watch. When a passerby asked "Did you lose it here?" the man said "No" and when the other man asked "Then why are you looking here?" he answered "Because the light's better here."

I discussed with this client how she could find a more discriminating approach, and we agreed that first she could decide what kind of person she would like to meet, then figure out where that person would be. Any city is likely to have many possibilities. My client, who liked tennis, joined a tennis club. Going to a gathering where one has a real interest increases the chances of finding others with something in common. And even if one does not make friends, the activity can still be enjoyable.

If one circulates among groups and meetings only with an eye out for eligible singles, one may come home disappointed. One woman took a class in finance because she was sure there would be more men than women in the class. There were, but she was too bored and confused by the lectures to start a meaningful conversation with the knowledgeable men, and soon dropped out. Another woman took an automobile mechanics class in order to meet men, only to find that all the members were women like herself. But learning about the workings of her car turned out to be very valuable. Since many colleges and schools offer extension or evening classes, it should not be hard to find a course that one can really enjoy. Some subjects, such as folk dancing or geology field trips, offer more chances to socialize than others.

Counselors must bear in mind, however, that financial constraints may limit a client's ability to take part in appropriate activities. At the same time, saying "I can't afford it" may be an excuse, and we can be alert to the possibility of the "Why don't you, yes but" game as a cover. I have often seen it played in a group where members are offering good suggestions. When Gretchen said that she wanted to meet more people, one group member said, "Why don't you take dancing lessons? You meet lots of people that way." Gretchen answered "Oh, I can't afford it." Another member said, "I think the YWCA gives really inexpensive lessons." Gretchen countered "Oh, that's much too far away." Another member of the group suggested "I think there's a branch in the north end where you live." Gretchen said, "Well, it sounds like a good idea, but I just can't find good sitters." Another woman offered "My children are all grown. I wouldn't mind sitting at your house once a week for a while." Gretchen ended the game with "That's awfully nice of you, but I really don't like to go out alone in the evening." Is this skilled "Yes, but" player really unable to invest in a class, or is she afraid of taking a risky step into unknown territory alone?

Even with the support of a group, people like Gretchen may still be too fearful to seek new social connections and too afraid of rejection. Research has underscored the obvious—that people who already had friends outside the marriage make a better adjustment after dissolution than those without a network (Levinger and Moles, 1979). The dilemma for lonely people is that the very ones most in need of friends are the ones least likely to find them. They never had to venture out alone during the marriage, so they may do nothing but go to work, come home, and sit by the television, hoping that Prince or Princess Charming will knock on the door. It is helpful to encourage small steps such as inviting a neighbor in for a cup of coffee or going to a meeting about an interesting subject. During the marriage people may have dropped their single friends long ago, and just making a telephone call to an almost forgotten friend can be rewarding. One divorcee found that calling up old friends just to chat often resulted in a dinner invitation. After a divorce, people may suddenly find that they have a good deal in common with divorced friends they formerly ignored. One woman reported that finding just one other divorced friend was a turning point. She said she began to come to life when she renewed contact with a woman whose marriage had ended in a similar way. Both husbands had left for younger women. Each divorcee had two children of school age so picnics, swimming, and trips to the zoo gave the mothers a social time while the children played together. Having one person to go out with can make all the difference between staying at home, hoping that something will happen, and taking the initiative to make it happen.

Some clients build up the courage to go to a singles' meeting, hoping to meet new people. When no one comes up and says hello, they sit down, thus making it more difficult for those who are circulating around to start a conversation. They may go home disgruntled, not realizing that many of the others are also waiting for someone else to make the first move. They, too, may be shy rather than uncaring. For clients willing to try again, we can provide some work on social skills. "Don't sit down!" can be good advice. One woman who gave a cocktail party decided to remove the chairs so that the guests would have to move around and talk to one another. With role playing, clients can practice simple greetings, like "Hello, I'm new here. Have you been here before?" Or a remark about the surroundings—"This is an attractive room, isn't it?" can hardly be out of place. Even the old standby, the weather, can provide an opening. After the meeting begins, of course, it is appropriate to sit down and one could practice saying "Shall we sit down?" or at a more advanced level "Will you sit over here with me?" Playing the role of the stranger, the counselor might respond in various ways, cordial and otherwise, to inoculate the client against gruff answers and provide an opportunity to practice responding to a pleasant suggestion or to a rebuff.

While many women have trouble taking the initiative, men can be just as fearful of rejection. A young woman who braved a singles' dance because she loved dancing noticed that many of the men sat for long periods surveying the scene, which meant that a good many women were never asked to dance. Why come to a dance, she wondered, if they don't want to dance, so she asked some of the men. One said "I have to have a few drinks before I get up my courage." Another sat back and said "Just window-shopping." The next man said he could not dance well and was afraid a partner would make fun of him. A more positive answer was given by a man who said "It's a good place to relax. I don't dance, but I get acquainted with people. I sit and talk with them. I've made new friends that way." The fifth man gave a vivid description of his fears. "You go to a table where a lot of women are sitting, and you stand there and ask one of them to dance and she turns you down" he said. "There you are, with everybody looking at you, and you'd feel foolish asking another one. She might turn you down, too. So you go back and sit down." Social anxiety is not limited to women.

For both men and women cognitive restructuring may reduce their fear of rejection. The anxious person may be "disasterizing" a small rebuff, like the man just described, who was probably telling himself "I'm not attractive. Nobody would want to dance with me. I might as well go home." A counselor could ask for proof of these statements and could ask the man to think of reasons why a woman might refuse a dance. She could be tired. Her feet could hurt. She might be afraid that she could not dance well enough to follow him. She might be very shy herself. Psychologists have studied the problems of shyness, and both counselors and clients may profit from reading *Shyness* by Philip Zimbardo (1977) and *Making Contact* by Arthur Wassmer (1978).

Developing social skills and combating shyness can increase self-confidence, which is probably the key to achieving satisfying social relationships. Developing other kinds of competence can also add to the feeling of autonomy. One middle-aged man who took all his meals in restaurants after his divorce insisted that this was a good way to meet women. Another reason he did not eat at home was that he never learned to cook or even toss a salad during the twenty-one years his wife had cared for him. He had not even tried to use the washing machine in his apartment. Not until the restaurant meals and laundry bills drained his finances did he reluctantly follow his counselor's suggestions. He was pleasantly surprised to find that he was quite capable of following cookbook directions and could actually produce acceptable meals. He began to feel proud of his new accomplishments and soon forgot his fear that the washing machine was an incomprehensible mechanical monster. Since most people after a dissolution find that they must do many tasks formerly in their spouse's department, rather than bemoan the extra work, they can focus on the benefits — new skills mean that they are more capable and more in control.

Not only household accomplishments but also achievement in a paid job can enrich the life of a newly single person. A woman who has never worked outside her home may need the help of a vocational counselor or a Displaced Homemaker program before she can find an appropriate career. Counselors can use the Strong-Campbell Interest Inventory or the Career Assessment Inventory to throw light on the kinds of work that would interest the client. (Both are listed in the bibliography.) I sometimes suggest *What Color Is Your Parachute?* by Richard Bolles (1986) for people who are undecided about a vocation. Clients who are working but dissatisfied with their jobs can be encouraged to take a look at other possibilities. They can list things that they like to do and ways that their favorite hobbies or pastimes might be converted into paying enterprises. Counselors need to be aware of their own biases about jobs. Since we are professional people, it may be hard to understand how a less educated person can enjoy and gain a sense of accomplishment from being a housewife, typist, or truck driver. But sometimes the suffering of divorce and the rethinking of values may inspire a person to find an occupation with more meaning. Increased sensitivity to their own and others' feelings makes some people dissatisfied with a job that has little social value. I have known several women who went to social work school after a divorce and at least one man whose divorce so changed his thinking that he decided to study for the ministry.

Those who for one reason or another have to remain in less than satisfying jobs may be encouraged to find volunteer work that provides enjoyment and a feeling of usefulness. Working with others gives greater opportunities for congenial friendships than just going to meetings as a passive observer. In one Parents Without Partners chapter, the officers and board members had to be replaced frequently since working together led to several marriages and resignations from the organization.

With or without counseling, and with or without coming to terms with the dissolution, the majority of divorced people eventually find a new partner, although more men remarry than women. More women remain single than men for several reasons. Death comes earlier for men, and men are usually attracted to younger women. This leaves many older women inevitably single. Perhaps the recent trend toward marriages of older women to younger men may be a sign of our liberation from sexual stereotypes and it will certainly reduce the number of women who spend lonely years as widows.

For those who feel that life is hardly worthwhile without a partner, it may take a long time to give up the belief that they are incomplete as single people. Certainly it is gratifying to have a supportive person with whom to share one's life, but this is different from believing that a partner is an absolute necessity. Too many people expect that a mate can meet every need, and it is useful to remind them that they can do much on their own to make their lives more rewarding, and that friends, children, and colleagues can provide a good deal of sharing and enjoyment as replacements for the lost partner. We can keep stressing the idea that no one is responsible for our happiness except ourselves, and that the more we can assume responsibility for enriching our own lives, the more we will have to offer to others. Clients who do not have to depend on other people will be more attractive to interesting eligibles of the opposite sex, especially to those who want someone who has interests other than just getting married.

Once clients have developed some postdivorce confidence, have found some friendships, and are engaged in interesting work, they will probably find leisure activities without a counselor's help. I have worked with a group of women, all well past middle-age and most of them divorced, who have found great enjoyment in putting on little plays that they rehearse in an acting class. They take their skits to retirement homes, senior centers, schools, and churches. One of their plays, called *Lifers,* written by their director, Toni Douglass (1984), is based on their own life experiences. In a scene called "Living Alone" five women speak in turn.

> **Polly:** They're all gone now. My parents, my children, my husband. After years and years in a house full of people, now I live alone. No one to take care of me. Did I say no one to take care of me? Why, I . . .
>
> **Margaret:** (*Dressed in a robe*) I took care of them! Now I don't have to get up early and get breakfast for anyone. I don't have to get up at all, if I don't want to. But I do want to, because I can have anything I want for breakfast. (*Produces huge ice cream container, and starts to eat.*)
>
> **Jana:** (*Dressed in a housecoat*) I can read the entire morning paper. I can leave it on the floor. I can dress when I please. Come to think of it, I don't have to dress at all, I can walk around the house undressed. (*Starts to undress, remembers audience and thinks better of it.*)
>
> **Sara:** (*Dressed in scruffy pants and shirt*) I can fill all the closets with my things and all the bookshelves with my books. I can go on a trip without waiting for somebody else to get a vacation. I don't have to call up if I'm late getting home for dinner. Don't have to feel guilty if it's leftovers again. I can sing badly, and dance to the radio. (*Begins a suggestive dance.*)
>
> **Ruth:** (*Dressed in caftan*) I can come in as late as I want to and read until 4 a.m. I can read while I eat, or watch television during dinner, which I never allowed the children to do. I can sleep catty-corner in the double bed, and last night when the cream pie was so good, I just picked up the dish and licked it! (*Licks pieplate.*)
>
> **Polly:** You know what I like best of all? I don't have to worry about my God-damned manners! (*All belch*)*

For this lively group, living alone is not all bad. If counseling can open new doors for people like these women, none of whom had done any acting before, then many others can also find new directions. And if we can help people start optimistically on the postdivorce stage of their lives, we can be satisfied.

---

*Reprinted with permission from "Lifers," copyright 1984 by Toni Douglass.

10
Counseling for Remarriage

When Elsa was about to graduate from college she took her fiance home to meet her parents for the first time. She did not tell them that she and Nick had been living together for a year because they were conservative and she thought they would disapprove. Ironically, at the end of the visit, Elsa's mother said "Your father and I like Nick, but we want you to be very sure. We think it would be a good idea for you to live with him for a while before you marry him. That way you'll really get to know him." Many have followed this kind of advice before marrying and many before remarrying. While living together before remarriage does not necessarily promise a happy life, it can be a good choice.

Whether people live together or not, most of those entering a second marriage want to avoid the trauma of another dissolution. Still, about half will be divorced a second time, and a few will experience third and fourth dissolutions. Some jump into second unions without any understanding of what pulled the first one apart. Some have not finished grieving over their divorce, and many harbor loving or resentful feelings toward their first wife or husband and often marry hastily to relieve their loneliness.

Clergymen and -women very often give premarriage counseling before a wedding, and some churches offer workshops or weekend retreats for couples. Although these programs may deter a small number from unwise choices, more often they are too late to be of much help. They are probably more apt to cement a good relationship than to prevent a poor one.

Some people, after an unfortunate first marriage, come to counseling for help in figuring out how to ensure that the second try will be more lasting than the first. Although we cannot ensure anything, we can help these thoughtful people explore why the first marriage did not last and help them learn more appropriate ways of choosing a partner and nurturing a marriage. They may be aware that they married too young before they knew what they really wanted in their adult lives, or that they married to spite their parents, or because of pregnancy, or to get away from an unhappy home situation. People do not usually enter second marriages for these reasons, but they need to examine their tendency to repeat the pattern. A woman who married to spite her parents may wish to remarry to spite the spouse who left her. A man who ran away from home rather than face his problems may remarry hastily to run away from the unpleasantness of living alone, instead of putting energy into action to improve his situation. I have seen several divorcees with children and an inadequate income who jumped at the chance to marry a solvent man as an escape from their troubles, without giving much thought to the man's other qualities. Or a custodial father may be so in need of a mother for his children (and possibly himself) that he marries the first likely woman he meets.

Some counselees may find that the first marriage was based on rescue operations. The best example of this is the woman who marries one alcoholic after another, either because she thinks she can rehabilitate him or because she enjoys the role of the magnanimous helper. Counselors can help rescuers see how they often become resentful victims and nagging persecutors when their efforts turn futile. At the same time the alcoholic, who does not believe he needs help, feels increasingly put down and resentful. As anger on both sides escalates, often the marriage collapses.

A similar pattern may emerge in cases involving physical abuse. One of my clients, Nathan, found himself stuck in the triangular trap after he married a young woman to rescue her from her physically abusive first husband. His marriage ended after the unappreciative wife returned several times to the abuser, which placed Nathan in the angry victim role, then the persecutor role. Nathan had been considering a second marriage to a woman who had become pregnant by another man, but in counseling he saw the noble rescuer pattern in himself just in time to avoid a repetition.

Other marriages have foundered because one or both parties feel inadequate, unable to take responsibility, or excessively dependent. During courtship a prospective husband or wife may have seemed sturdy as a rock, but everyone has some dependency wishes, and this seemingly strong person may also have hoped to find a caretaker. If both partners want to lean, the marriage will be about as unstable as the proverbial house built on sand. Or if the more independent person is as strong as he or she appears, annoyance at the clinging partner may grow into contempt and finally lead to a dissolution. A dependent person may have to spend a long time in counseling before enough self-confidence is built up to prevent another leaning marriage. Counseling can help such clients realize that no matter how much they needed care and nurturing as children, they are now adults with the resources to provide a good deal of caring for themselves, and they do not need to behave like helpless children in order to be loved. It is usually harder for men than for women to admit that they want to be taken care of. Recent studies of batterers suggest that some of these men have hidden their dependency wishes because they are ashamed. Then when the grow increasingly angry at their wives for not gratifying their unspoken wants, as well as annoyed at themselves for having "unmanly" desires, they let their frustration explode in a physical attack.

In unraveling the mystery of why the choices of a mate who seems so right on the wedding day can lead to such unhappy endings, we can be alert to competitive attitudes that can gradually erode a relationship. Larry was a star athlete and president of the graduating class in his small town high school. Later he kept up his competitive interests by captaining a championship bowling team. His teammates married their high school sweethearts, but Larry waited until he found a real prize. Marie, a young woman from the city, was a college graduate with a good job in a social agency. Larry basked in the glory of her accomplishments, which were far above those of his friends' small town brides. Larry was a college dropout in a dead-end job, and while he said he was pleased when Marie was promoted to supervisor, he felt eclipsed at the party in her honor. Later he felt put down when she wanted to discuss child welfare instead of listening to his bowling scores. Soon, having an accomplished wife no longer satisfied his competitive drive. He was competing with her but not winning. Finally he left Marie for a less educated woman to whom he could feel superior. Had he come for counseling before his second marriage he might have realized how his need to excel was motivating his poor choice of partners.

Marie, on the other hand, did come for counseling after the divorce. How did she happen to marry a man who did not share her strong interest in social concerns? Although she was a good student and attractive, Marie was quiet and studious and had always felt like an ugly duckling compared to her lively older sister Monica, who went from May Queen to Prom Queen, always in demand for dates. Larry was tall and handsome, the kind of popular man who usually noticed Monica and ignored Marie. For several years her exhilaration at being chosen outweighed her disappointment in Larry's limited interests, and it was hard for her to admit that she had made a mistake. In counseling Marie was able to develop a more realistic concept of herself as a likeable person, and to cease seeing herself in Monica's shadow. If she marries again she will likely no longer need another person to help her make up for her imagined inadequacies.

Although many people who want help on making a better choice next time will insist on reviewing the faults of their previous spouses, we need to put the emphasis on the reasons for their self-defeating choice in the first place. Only after they understand why they made unsuitable choices are clients ready to look at a prospective partner sensibly. Many have never seriously considered what they value most in their lives or what they would value most highly in a marriage. They may not realize that a value is a chosen way of life that one *acts* upon, rather than just *thinking* about it. In order to help them with this, I have my clients make two lists — one of the values most important in their lives and the other of what would be most important in their marriages. Several inventories are available to help people sort out their priorities. Dr. Milton Rokeach has devised The Values Survey, (1978) which lists such values as pleasure, health, true friendship, a world at peace, and wisdom. These are to be arranged in order of priority from one to eighteen. Dr. Rokeach's second list consists of adjectives ranging from ambitious to courageous to self-controlled, and these too are to be arranged in the order in which they are valued. When clients make up their own lists of what they consider most important in a marriage, they may include companionship, fidelity, intimate communication, shared religion, enjoyment of children, and so on. If two people take the same test, they will certainly gain insight into each other's values, and can measure how well they agree.

Richard Stuart and Barbara Jacobson, in their book *Second Marriage* (1985), describe some different exercises they use in premarital counseling. In one of these exercises prospective partners are asked to rate the positive and negative qualities of the former spouse and the new partner as well as to rate their own positive and negative traits. They then compare their ratings. If both the past and future mates have the same negative traits, this is a warning signal. If a person does not find a new marriage partner, looking over these lists of values will show them which values they can obtain by themselves and which ones a marriage can provide. People may be surprised to find that values they consider worthwhile often do not require a marriage partner.

For those who choose to remarry, discussing attitudes about what they consider important in a marriage may prevent some mistakes. Getting married without understanding how the other person feels about important aspects of life would be like going blindfolded through an obstacle course. Misunderstandings are likely if a person does not know when the partner wants verbal or physical expression of affection, or how the partner feels about who takes the initiative in sex. Some couples easily arrive at a good understanding by trial and error, but other matters may be more difficult for them to discuss. I remember a letter to Dear Abby in which a young woman described her romantic affair. With her low income she could not afford her contraceptive pills and wanted the young man to help pay for them. Her problem was that she did not know him well enough yet to talk about money!

Infidelity is probably not on the minds of people about to marry unless they have encountered it before, but frank discussion of just what they would tolerate in the way of time spent with members of the opposite sex can clarify where the limits are. Discussion of how partners feel about having children, and about how to deal with each other's children from a previous marriage is important. To some, taking inventories and other premarital tests may seem cold, calculating, and unromantic, but these exercises may help keep the romantic bloom in their marriage, or in some cases, prevent an unfortunate mismatch.

Before remarriage most people are good at pleasing each other and hiding unfortunate personality traits such as irresponsibility, a poorly controlled temper, or irrational jealousy, which are bound to surface when people share their living space. Counselors can suggest that to uncover some of these aspects of behavior the future partners plan to see each other under all kinds of circumstances—indoor, outdoor, formal, informal, with children, with relatives, with friends, and at times when they are frustrated, angry, or depressed. Covering all these bases naturally points to the importance of sufficient time before two people get married. June took her fiance to a party where Mac seemed to mix well with her friends, but he was furious with her afterward because she had enjoyed a conversation with a single man she had not seen for years. Mac's jealousy was so out of proportion that June decided against marrying him and considered herself fortunate to have discovered his jealous rage in time.

Mac's jealousy is one example of the kinds of problems people would do well to discuss in detail before they marry. They could be specific about their tolerance for everything from lunch with a friend of the opposite sex to having flirtations. Jealousy can apply to same-sex friends as well. I have counseled couples where the wife's desire to spend an evening with women friends was intolerable to the husband, or the husband's intention to resume men's club activities left his wife feeling jealous and abandoned.

One woman fell for the apparently gentle nature of a young man who often sent her flowers, but saw another side of him one day as they drove in traffic. As another car started to edge in front of them, the young man shouted "Get the Hell out of there, damn you! Why don't you take a day off and learn how to drive?" My client was shocked and after several more outbursts she decided not to risk having his wrath turned against her, flowers or no flowers. Another client fell out of love soon after meeting her fiance's family. She knew that Lee's father had deceived his wife with extramarital affairs, but she was sure that Lee disliked his father's behavior and was very different from him. After a few Sundays spent with Lee's parents, my client saw how much Lee enjoyed some of his father's hurtful jokes against his mother. Seeing the similarity between the two men, she soon broke the engagement. One man found that his fiance was thoroughly bored when they visited his mother to the point of leaving early in a discourteous way. After she announced that from now on he could visit his mother alone, Keith had second thoughts about going through with the marriage.

While it seems obvious to most people that they had better have realistic information about how a new partner will behave in matters of money, children, and intimacy, many overlook other less weighty but often significant behaviors such as personal habits. Having dirty nails, procrastinating, always being late, and leaving dirty dishes on the counter are the kinds of annoyances that need to be observed and weighed. Some expectations are never discussed because people assume that the other person wants the same things. Lillian was so thrilled at marrying Steve that she moved happily into his tiny apartment, telling herself they would get a house later. After some months she found that Steve had no interest in taking on the responsibilities of a house and yard. Lillian could not give up her dream of owning a house and kept at Steve until he reluctantly bought one. Steve disliked the move and shirked the yard chores, and Lillian began to nag and resent him. When last seen, this marriage was very unstable.

A man and a woman, even when they are from similar backgrounds and hold similar values, are not identical twins. They will not have identical tastes in housing, interior decorating, food, or recreation. I am sometimes asked, "How important is it for us to have common interests? I like to go jogging and he doesn't" or "What happens if she wants to go to concerts and I would rather go to a funny movie?" If these differences have been invisible before marriage, the couple will be in for some disappointments. Rosemary is an example. She loved to dance and during their courtship Edwin frequently took her to dances, but after they married he refused to dance any more. "I don't really like it. I just did it to get you to marry me," he said. They are still married, perhaps as a tribute to Rosemary's sense of humor and tolerance for frustration, two traits I think are closely related. Both indicate that one is flexible enough to change one's views and look at things in a favorable rather than a gloomy light.

Sometimes differences can enrich rather than pull apart a marriage. A person who never thought of going to a jazz concert may develop a liking for it after being coaxed to a concert by the partner. A husband may have no desire to take up his wife's hobby of painting but may encourage her and enjoy hanging her pictures on their walls. A wife may be glad to have her husband play poker with his friends on Tuesday evenings while she goes to her bridge club. A man who hates shopping with his wife may be happy to stay home and putter about the house while she spends Saturday at the sales. Unfortunately it is the opposite scenario I more often hear. "He never wants to go shopping with me. He makes me go alone. We never do anything together. I think he likes to be away from me." Or, "My wife spends all her time painting or going to her art classes. I think she would rather do that than talk to me. I feel lonely and left out." It is not the difference in interests but what the people tell themselves about differences that can make or break a marriage. If they think "It's good for my spouse to have an interesting hobby" the activity will not be a problem. As in Larry and Marie's case, it was not their different interests that destroyed their marriage, but the fact that Larry felt undermined when he compared himself to Marie.

In preparing for a second marriage, it is helpful to explore not only the reasons for the first choice, but the story of what happened to change the marvelous wedding day optimism into the sad decision to divorce. Uncovering harmful interactions would be easier if we could see both people, and avoid a one-sided account, but after a dissolution it is not likely that a couple will come in together. Certainly we can look for any unreasonable expectations that were brought to the marriage. Some clients expected that getting married would meet all their needs and were disappointed when the spouse had some activities on the agenda other than catering to the partner's wishes. One impossible expectation is that my husband or wife will love me no matter what I do. Under this mistaken notion, people have been critical, neglectful, or outright abusive, secure (they think) in the steadfast love of their partner. Some hold the common belief that marriage is an end in itself, which will produce happiness, rather than marriage being a means to achieve a happy life. I avoid telling people to work on their relationship. Rather, I remind them that their marriage needs nurturing, a more positive connotation than work. The idea that love is a thing that is just there, rather than a daily activity, will damage any union. Many marriages end because the parties think love means you do not have to ask for what you want, or you never get angry at your mate, or you never have to apologize for mistakes. Equally illusory is the hope that problems will go away if we do nothing about them. "He won't hit me again, I'm sure" or "She'll get over her drinking—she promised" are the deceptively hopeful ideas that help ill-fated marriages go downhill.

If the first marriage has not already shattered these beliefs, we can ask clients to think about why they hold these ideas, and can use logic to help them disprove and discard them. Some shoulds about gender roles, for example, cause dissension. Some people still assign traditional roles to men and women. One man I saw prided himself because he held two jobs in order to provide well for his wife and children. He was dumbfounded when his wife took the children and left. She was tired of sitting home alone every evening and tired of his total lack of interaction with the children, who were in bed when he left in the morning and when he came home late at night. He called her unappreciative and looked for a new wife. He was not open to learning that in a good marriage the husband's emotional presence is as important as his good provider role, if not more so.

Some clients are willing to accept their share of the responsibility for the demise of the relationship. Anyone who has been through a divorce does not have to be told that conflicts are inevitable when two people live together. If two quarreling people reveal their feelings honestly, they will learn new dimensions of each other, and this understanding may increase good feelings. I have described methods for a divorced pair to deal with conflicts and anger in Chapter 7. When married couples fight there is a difference because they are committed to each other and, unlike divorced people, both want to kiss and make up in the end. In premarital counseling they can get over their fear of expressing anger toward each other, as they learn that anger is not usually lethal, and that even hating each other temporarily shows that they are very much involved. Indifference, not hatred, is the opposite of love. To help clients learn constructive ways to handle conflicts we can remind them that all of us are vulnerable, and if self-esteem is not belittled in a quarrel the outcome will be much more favorable than if people stab each other with insults and threats. If one person feels demeaned the marriage is weakened because the other partner cannot feel secure and loved while the disparaged one is dejected and sullen. Both need to feel sure of the other's commitment. And both may need to look at and dispute the irrational idea that anyone can be threatened or coerced into being more loving.

Some conflicts can be easily settled using methods that children have known for years. Taking turns and bargaining can help in the dispute I hear about most often — how to divide up the housework chores equitably. Some couples decide that the person who earns the most money should have less work to do at home. Some think that each should do half of the chores because they spend an equal amount of time at their outside jobs, and others divide housework on the basis of who does it best. Listing chores does not always get the work done, and frequent conflicts occur because one does his or her share and the other does not. An old trick is to fumble the job so badly that the other partner takes it over, grumbling all the way. Since housework can be such a source of contention, couples would do well to discuss it ahead of time. They can become clear about their feelings in the matter and share them with each other. Probably washing dishes or dusting furniture has an entirely different meaning for each person. One may see housework as distasteful servant's work. The other may see a clean, orderly house as a necessary part of the ambience of an emotionally satisfying home. Understanding each other's perception may help get rid of sexist prejudices or childish attitudes toward housework based on what mother used to do. Counseling may reveal that the foot-dragger is upset about something else that the spouse is doing, and is acting out this resentment through passive non-cooperation. Spelling out the complaint openly is the only way to improve the situation.

A client might say "But I can't tell her that I really don't like the way she cooks! I might hurt her feelings." Fear of hurting feelings can cloud many issues and perpetuate a good deal of annoyance not only in families but in many human encounters. Dear Abby columns often feature people who cannot tell neighbors to keep their dogs at home or cannot tell a friend not to visit at an inconvenient time as though a tactfully expressed request would end a friendship. (A request is certainly more acceptable than a demand.) In a marriage dislikes and requests for change will have to be expressed, preferably in private, at a time when the partner is feeling well and things are calm. Even if the person is temporarily wounded, hurt feelings are not terminal, and may even be educational.

Counseling for remarriage is not exclusively about conflict management.

Equally important is emphasis on giving each other positive reinforcement, that marvelous motivator so strangely underused by people who want someone else to change. If a spouse does not respond to simple requests for change, it may be that the partner has expressed no appreciation for previous changes. Many of us say "Thank you" to an apathetic store clerk more consistently than to our own wives and husbands. I am reminded of a cartoon in which a husband comes home and presents his wife with a bouquet of flowers. She stands there and says "Well, it's about time!" Some counselors suggest that couples give each other at least three positive strokes each day, in words, good deeds, or physical affection. This may sound like advice in a popular woman's magazine but it is scientifically sound. If a client finds it difficult to express positive feelings then we can explore the underlying resentment, or possibly some outdated injunction that is inhibiting spontaneity. Perhaps the uptight person feels that expressing affection makes one vulnerable or that it is silly.

A client contemplating a second marriage to a person who is caring for children from a previous marriage or a custodial parent who wants to marry someone who has never had children or who is bringing another group of youngsters into the home is in a difficult situation. These combinations are very common since the number of stepfamilies has increased enormously in recent years. Although stepmothers have had a very bad reputation since the days of Cinderella, stepfathers actually are much more likely to be guilty of child abuse. While not condoning abuse, we may sympathize with the frustration that leads up to the abuse as men try to find ways to fill the difficult and ambiguous stepfather role. Adding even one child to a dyad increases the number of interactions from two to six. If several children are involved for both partners, and if each parent has dealings with a previous spouse and possibly that person's new husband or wife and children, the logistics of this megafamily becomes exceedingly complex. Research on stepfamilies has proliferated and two books available for counselors are *Stepfamilies: A Guide to Working with Stepparents and Stepchildren* (Visher and Visher 1979) and *Treating the Remarried Family* (Sager et al. 1983).

In the simplest case I have known, a man with a small daughter married a woman who had no children. When Amy, who lived with her mother, visited every other weekend, her stepmother was delighted to entertain her and sew for her. Amy's mother was not only glad to have the dresses but was pleased with the new relationship. She realized that a child cannot have too many loving parents and all went well. Not many are so idyllic. In a remarriage where one child is involved, the child may be jealous because his or her exclusive relationship with mother or father is now threatened by an intruder in the house, or the new spouse may be jealous of the child who takes up so much of the partner's attention. In any divorce having a sibling to confide in can be very helpful to children.

Since jealousy of stepparents and stepchildren is a likely issue after remarriage, counselors can help by pointing out that love is not a finite quantity. Just as parents can love three or four or even ten children, albeit not equally, a child in a healthy environment can grow to love three or four parents. It is important to stress that love for a new stepfather or stepmother in no way diminishes a child's love for the natural parents, and children can be assured that their father's or mother's new partner and new stepchildren cannot take away the love for their own offspring.

In the most complex cases when two parents remarry the children may acquire a new stepmother and stepfather, two new sets of stepsiblings, some new half-siblings, and if the older generation is still living, eight grandparents instead of the usual four. Family counseling in such a situation would require an auditorium! I recall a story in which a family moved from Minnesota to a New York suburb and became the only intact nuclear family on the block. The boy felt deprived on Christmas with his small collection of presents when the other children displayed their enormous hoards of bicycles, watches, and roller skates from "my first stepmother," "my second stepfather's wife," "my stepgrandfather."

Since we live in the age of divorce where a large percentage of children will spend time in a single parent home, Constance Ahrons (1979) reminds us that two parents are usually involved, and suggests that we use the term *binuclear family* instead of *single parent family*. Certainly the existence of the other parent can be a complication for the remarried family if the divorced couple have not diluted their old ties and achieved a more objective working relationship. It will be hard to adjust to a new husband or wife without jealousy if she or he is still in an affectionate relationship with the previous spouse. Even more difficult is the situation if the new partner is still angry with the ex-partner and still wrangling and preoccupied over problems of money and children. Counseling to finish the dissolution process before remarriage is necessary in these cases.

Very often couples do not foresee all the disruptions and adjustments that remarriage involves. Some people, forgetting how the arrival of a child can upset routines, have the fantasy that the sudden acquisition of a stepchild will be easy. When I led a therapy group of stepfathers and their wives, all of whom had problem children, they discovered that they had much in common (Mowatt 1972). The stepparent role is completely lacking in guidelines, and all of the men were perplexed about how to show affection to their often sullen stepchildren, and were confused about how far to go in making rules and punishing the children like real fathers. The mothers, who had been struggling on their own for several years before remarrying, had imagined that the reconstituted family would solve all their problems. At last they would have a complete family again. They wanted the children and the stepfathers to like, if not love one another, but sometimes defeated their own purpose by pushing too hard to get them to do things together. One mother thought that playing table games together would help the family become cohesive. Since her new husband did not like the games and argued with the children about the rules, the plan was a disaster. In one family the mother eagerly tried to promote a good relationship between her fourteen-year-old daughter and her new husband, Gil. She told the girl to ask her stepfather to take her to the movies. Then she took her husband aside and told him that the daughter wanted to go and suggested that it would be nice for him to take her. In the car Gil and the girl began to talk and found that neither cared about the movie and neither wanted to miss their favorite television program. They told each other about the mother's conniving, went back in the house, and enjoyed popcorn and television together. While this situation ended happily, counselors can caution the natural parents about letting the new relationship work itself out without too much interference.

It was much more difficult for the mothers in my group to avoid interfering when the stepfathers wanted to discipline the children. The women insisted their new husbands take on a real father's responsibilities but they usually rushed to the children's defense if he scolded or criticized the children. This left the new fathers in difficult positions, and some gave up enforcing any rules. Instead the stepfathers nagged their wives when the children ran wild.

Sometimes habits that could not have been foreseen caused dissension. One strict stepfather insisted that the children keep their shoes on at all times in the house even though their mother had always allowed them to run around in their socks. Since there was no apparent compromise solution, the couple never stopped arguing about this. In another family, the children and the mother had been courted by the future stepfather with a round of trips, picnics, gifts and celebrations. After the marriage he reverted to a more authoritarian attitude. He locked up his stereo, tapes, and large television, and resented it when his wife spent money on the children's ski lessons. None of the couples in my group had planned ahead about how to handle these important matters, and all felt relieved and supported to find that others had similar problems. When the stepfathers learned to blame themselves and their wives less and their ambiguous role more, they could relax more easily with the stepchildren. And the mothers grew more tolerant of their husbands as they became aware of their own contributions to the family's troubles.

Different problems may arise when a noncustodial parent takes a new partner. One father, looking forward to introducing his children to his new wife on their first visit after his honeymoon, was dismayed when his former wife demanded that he see the children without his new wife present. He honored this demand at first, fearing that he might lose the visits entirely, but eventually the children's mother had to accept the fact that his remarriage was there to stay. Other parents refuse to allow visits when the former wife or husband is living, unmarried, with a partner, or in a homosexual relationship, citing religious or moral scruples. Long and expensive court battles often follow that are particularly painful for the vulnerable children.

If a person who lives with his or her own children marries a noncustodial parent, the latter's child, whose visits are limited to every other weekend, may be confused and jealous. "How come Daddy spends all that time with kids that aren't even his, and so little time with me?" is the understandable complaint. When we work with these parents we may find that the two groups of children are always merged in family activities. These parents can be helped to see the importance of giving as much time as possible to their own children as well as seeing each child alone. How else can there be any real communication? A father may feel that he does not have enough time to divide up this way, but if he can manage half an hour with each child on every visit, the investment will result in a better attitude on the part of his youngsters and a smoother transition to the blended family he wants.

Sometimes stepparenting leads to interfamily disputes very difficult for counselors to untangle. Two adolescent boys, who lived with their permissive father, slouched on the couch with their feet on the coffee table whenever they visited their mother. Her strict new husband, Albert, and his well-behaved children were horrified at the boys' sloppiness and scratching of furniture. Albert tried to teach them manners and heaped blame on the boys' natural father. When the two angry teenagers then objected to visiting at mother's, the father, who did not want to give up his childfree weekends, blamed their mother. The mother criticized Albert and Albert told the boys' father to "Get lost!" To intervene in such a situation would be difficult for a counselor who cannot see all the parties involved. Still it is useful to work with as many family members as possible to help them see that everybody wants a pleasant, conflict-free family. They might begin by brainstorming ways to improve the situation. They might think of having the boys take off their shoes in the house or planning some outdoor activities where neatness would not be an issue. The parents could learn to express positive wishes and requests rather than criticizing, and could give positive reinforcement for even small acts of compliance. A counseling session with the boys, with encouragement to express their gripes, might uncover some hidden resentments, give them some relief, and diminish the need for passive-aggressive behavior in their mother's home.

Planning ahead cannot avoid all impasses (who could predict that taking shoes off in the house or eating ice cream cones in the living room would become a problem?). Before anyone moves into a home where children are already used to a set of routines, rules, and privileges, it is important for a couple to agree on the most crucial matters. We can ask the couple to consider how much of the family budget will go for children's allowances and other expenses and to discuss their policies on curfew, bedtimes, neatness, and chores. And if punishment is necessary, we can ask what will be used and who will apply it. After parents have divided up which behaviors will be the mother's responsibility and which the father's, we can remind them to stay out of each other's way. Forgetting this was the mistake so often made in the homes of my stepfamily group. The mother wanted the father to take charge of discipline, then interfered when he did. As in any organization, if one has the responsibility for a task, one needs the authority to do it.

In their book *Second Marriage* (1985), Stuart and Jacobson provide a list of child-related areas for couples to discuss before remarriage. Each person is to rate how important the area is (such as religious activity, clothes, use of telephone, respect for parents), note who is to be responsible for it, and write down who is to decide the rules in each matter. This list identifies preferences as well as prejudices, and I trust that this thorough preview will not cause people to give up entirely on the idea of stepping into a family. If it does, that may be a good thing, because stepparenting is as difficult as it can be rewarding.

Certainly people who choose second marriages, with or without children, can be more successful if they take the time to prepare themselves. Counselors can help them understand what went into the choice of the first partner and what they wish to look for in a second relationship. If we can provide partners with tools for communicating well and settling disputes, they will be ready to create a more rewarding marriage the second time around.

11
Are There Solutions to Dissolution?

Counselors who have worked with people in unhappy marriages and unhappy divorces, and have seen children who have suffered in the fallout from their parents' separation, must wonder what we can do to prevent the emotional toll so many people are paying for these family break-ups. And the damage is not entirely personal. Society, too, is paying for the costs. Two families cannot live as cheaply as one, and incomes drop for the parents who care for the children. Because women earn much less than men, and because support payments are often inadequate or missing, society pays for low-income mothers in the form of Aid to Families with Dependent Children, subsidized housing, Medicaid, mental health services, and the legal costs of collecting support money. Even though funding for these services has unfortunately been cut in recent years, still all of us are paying for the costs of divorce.

In spite of the burdens, few people would mandate an end to dissolutions. Certainly to continue in a destructive marriage can bring more misery than ending it. Divorce can often be the necessary ticket to a better life in the future. While counseling can relieve the unhappiness after an unviable marriage ends, counselors can also do a good deal to prevent marriages that are not likely to endure.

First, counselors can use their expertise to help educate the public, especially the young, on the importance of looking before they leap into marriage. They can advocate the introduction or continuation of education for responsible sexuality in schools. Aware of the power of adolescents' hormones, we can work toward reducing the number of marriages based on pregnancy. Counselors can also advocate education for marriage and parenting in high schools, and in many cases can teach family life courses. Some of these include practical information on the realities of keeping house. Students may do research on the costs of food, rent, utilities, and furniture, and can compare them with the wages they can earn in the jobs available to them after high school. This comparison may be a sobering shock to the students. Learning the costs of having and raising a baby may influence young people to take contraception seriously. While I have no data on how many teenagers are deterred from early marriages by the kind of information just mentioned, we can hope that some will learn to enter into marriage carefully.

Since most people will eventually marry, psychology courses dealing with personality patterns, traits that interfere with a good partnership, and ways of resolving conflicts would be a step toward preventing inappropriate marriages and preserving more viable ones. Counselors are equipped to teach young people about the hazards of leaning on others, or of having to be "top dog," or of the need to rescue underdogs. Courses could emphasize the importance of independence, and the difference between leaving home to be independent versus achieving maturity by becoming responsible while still living at home. Students could be taught how to express anger in nondestructive ways as well as how to communicate good feelings. Assertiveness training and conflict management skills would also be useful. Counselors could offer to lecture in these classes or could advocate their inclusion in local schools.

Counselors can also play an effective part in educating people past high school age on making better marriage choices as well as making their existing marriages more satisfactory. Either in clinics or on their own, counselors can offer classes on preparation for marriage, and on marriage and divorce problems. Classes are much more acceptable than counseling for many people who refuse to see a therapist because they are afraid of being stigmatized as crazy. And classes, of course, can reach many more people in the community than counseling.

In spite of the best efforts at divorce prevention, dissolutions will continue to be with us, and we can be influential by cooperating with some of the institutions that have sprung up in response to the needs of the many divorced individuals. One of the first was Parents Without Partners, started in 1955 by two single parents who compared notes one day on how they coped with parenting alone. They placed an advertisement in New York's *Village Voice*, hoping to find a few others in the same predicament, and were amazed by the size of the crowd that came to the first meeting as well as the others who telephoned. The organization spread rapidly to other parts of the United States and Canada. It fills a real need by providing social occasions, children's activities, educational programs, and many other events for single parents in hundreds of communities. Parents Without Partners also has a national magazine, *The Single Parent*. Counselors can offer their expertise as lecturers and discussion group leaders to PWP chapters.

Counselors can provide similar services to the singles organizations that churches often sponsor. No longer shunning their many divorced members, some religious groups have organized singles clubs that offer education, social programs, and a supportive environment. If no such organizations are available counselors can help start them in local churches. Some service organizations such as the YMCA, YWCA, YMHA, and YWHA provide classes or support groups for single parents where counselors are valuable as leaders.

One church in Seattle sponsors a program called Divorce Lifeline that offers help for divorcing or recently divorced people through groups led by trained mental health professionals. Hundreds of people in the last ten years have joined these groups that meet one evening a week. Groups usually consist of eight or nine people who commit themselves to participating for three or six months with the option to renew their commitment. A study by Carol Henry (1981) shows that the group discussions help the members feel less depressed. They also gain more self-respect and get over some of their anger about the dissolution. Divorce Lifeline has three different locations in the greater Seattle area and new centers in British Columbia. Recently the program has added groups for adolescents and for children from ages six to twelve. Counselors could take the lead in starting a similar service in their communities.

Another interesting program in which counselors have played an important role is offered by the University Unitarian Church in Seattle. For sixteen years the Solo Series has drawn an audience of about fifty people each Sunday evening to hear a qualified speaker lecture on some aspect of single life. Topics include regaining self-esteem, establishing new relationships, and recovering from loss. Talks have dealt with jealousy, sexuality, parenting, fears, and many other subjects important to divorced and other unmarried men and women. Counselors are very willing to present a program for a small honorarium because the Solo Series is a good way to publicize a clinic or a private practice. This format could easily be followed in other cities where mental health professionals are available.

More politically active are the groups that advocate the rights of those affected by divorce. The National Organization for Women is interested in promoting the rights of women in divorce, and the National Congress for Men is an umbrella organization for the men's rights groups that have appeared in many states. A group pressing for the rights of grandparents in their children's divorces is also active. Counselors who agree with the agenda of one or another of these organizations can be influential in their programs. They can work toward fair divorce and custody laws, for effective methods of collecting child support and for ways of ensuring that noncustodial parents have access to their children. A list of relevant national organizations is in the appendix.

Counselors can promote the practice of mediation rather than litigation in their communities and can work with librarians to ensure the availability of the many self-help books, which may help divorcing people through the difficult territory. On a larger scale, it is up to society to recognize that the old ideal of the two-parent family, with mother caring for children at home and father at his outside job, is no longer the norm. Divorce is no longer the shameful exception—it is an important, ubiquitous institution that we need to provide for and accept. Several suggestions have been made to lessen the number of divorces and to alleviate their unfortunate effects. While marriage licenses cost only a few dollars and require only a short waiting period, divorce can cost hundreds of dollars and require months or even years to settle. It would seem that we have our priorities backwards. Reversing these requirements so that marriage licenses would cost several hundred dollars and require a waiting period of weeks or months might seem like an outlandish idea, but it might also ensure that the couple had the maturity to save for their goals and to delay gratification for a reasonable period of time. While I do not advocate a three-dollar, three-day divorce, I believe that the contrast between the two legal transitions reflects our society's laissez faire attitude toward a major life decision.

Divorce insurance is a possibility that has not received much attention. Couples might pay premiums during their marriage into a policy that would provide funds to pay attorneys and other expenses in case of divorce. The idea may horrify young couples, but there is a practical side to such a policy. Perhaps if it were called marriage insurance more people would find it acceptable. Another sensible suggestion is to require or at least encourage couples to take courses on the practical and emotional aspects of marriage before a marriage license is issued. Couples might even be required to take an oral or written test. Although some may see a test as an invasion of our civil liberties, still we all accept the need for passing a test before we can drive a car.

Our federal government has provided some funding for Displaced Homemaker services, for collecting child support, and for finding kidnapped children of divorce. Some states offer mediation and counseling for couples in dissolution. Movement in the direction of uniform divorce and child custody laws is gathering momentum. Still more needs to be done to help divorced people.

Since there is no way to ensure that every marriage will last a lifetime, we shall continue to grapple with the disasters of dissolution—the financial hardships, the emotional upheavals, the social disruption, and the injury to children. With the help of counselors, we are gradually finding ways to relieve these problems so that men and women can emerge with a better understanding of themselves and their marital choices. At the same time, our work can help reduce the pain and stigma of divorce and can guide the survivors toward happier lives.

Appendix
National Organizations

Many of these organizations can refer people to local chapters.

General

Divorce After 60
c/o Turner Geriatric Clinic, 1010 Wall St., University of Michigan, Ann Arbor, MI 48109

Divorce Anonymous (Self-help)
P.O. Box 5313, Chicago, IL 60680

National Association of Christian Singles
915 W. Wisconsin Ave., Suite 214, Milwaukee, WI 53233

National Committee for Fair Divorce and Alimony Laws
217 Broadway, Room 404, New York, NY 10007

North American Conference of Separated and Divorced Catholics
1100 Goodman St., Rochester, NY 14620

United States Divorce Reform
P.O. Box 243, Kenwood, CA 95452

For Parents

Committee for Mother and Child Rights
Box 481, Chappaqua, NY 10514

Fathers Are Forever
P.O. Box 4804, Panorama City, CA 91412

Fathers' Rights of America
P.O. Box 7596, Van Nuys, CA 91409

Joint Custody Association
10606 Wilkins Ave., Los Angeles, CA 90024

Mothers Without Custody
Box 602, Greenbelt, MD 20770

National Single Parent Coalition
225 Part Avenue, S., 7th floor, New York, NY 10003

National Society of Fathers for Child Custody and Divorce Law Reform
P.O. Box 010847, Flagler Station, Miami, FL 33101

Organization for the Enforcement of Child Support
119 Nicodemus Rd., Reisterstown, MD 21136

Parents and Children's Equality (PACE)
2054 Loma Linda Way S., Clearwater, FL 33575

Parents Sharing Custody
18401 Burbank Blvd., Suite 229, Tarzana, CA 91356

Parents Without Partners
7910 Woodmont Ave., Suite 1000, Bethesda, MD 20814

Single Dads' Hotline
P.O. Box 4842, Scottsdale, AZ 85258

For Men

America's Society of Separated and Divorced Men
575 Keep St., Elgin, IL 60120

Men's Rights Association
17854 Lyons, Forest Lake, MI 55025

National Congress for Men
P.O. Box 147, Mendham, NJ 07945

National Organization for Men
381 Port Ave. S., New York, NY 10016

For Women

Displaced Homemakers Network
1010 Vermont Ave., N.W., Suite 817, Washington, DC 20005

National Organization for Women (NOW)
1401 New York Ave. N.W., Suite 800, Washington, DC 20005–2102

Older Women's League (OWL)
1325 G St. N.W., LLB, Washington, DC 20005

Second Wives Association of North America
720 Spadina Ave., Suite 509, Toronto, Ontario, Canada M5S 2T9

For Grandparents

Foundation for Grandparenting
10 W. Hyatt Ave., Mt. Kisco, NY 10549

Grandparents Anonymous
c/o Encyclopedia of Associations, Gale Research Co., Book Tower, Detroit, MI 48226

Grandparents'/Children's Rights
5728 Bayonne Ave., Haslett, MI 48840

For Stepfamilies

Remarried Parents, Inc.
c/o Jack Pflaster, 102-20 67th Drive, Forest Hills, NY 11375

Stepfamily Association of America
28 Allegheny Ave., Suite 1307, Baltimore, MD 21204

Stepfamily Foundation
333 West End Ave., New York, NY 10023

Missing Children

Child Find
Box 277, New Paltz, NY 12561

Citizens' Committee to Amend Title 18 (Custodial parents whose children have been taken by noncustodial parents)
P.O. Box 936, Newhall, CA 91321

Find the Children
1811 West Olympic Blvd., Los Angeles, CA 90064

Missing Children Help Center
410 Ware Blvd., Suite 400, Tampa, FL 33619

Missing Children of America
P.O. Box 10-1938, Anchorage, AK 99510

For Children of Divorced Parents

National Council for Children's Rights, Inc.
2001 O St. N.W., Washington, DC 20036

Mediation Services

Academy of Family Mediators
1114 4th Ave., Suite IV, New York, NY 10003

Family Mediation Association
9308 Bulls Run Parkway, Bethesda, MD 20034

Bibliography

General

Adler, Alfred. *The Science of Living.* Garden City, New York: Garden City Publishing Company, 1929.
Ahrons, Constance R. "The Binuclear Family: Two Households, One Family." *Alternative Lifestyles.* 2 (1979):499–515.
———. "The Continuing Coparental Relationship between Divorced Spouses." *American Journal of Orthpsychiatry* 51 (3) (1981):415–428.
Bach, George. "Creative Exits: Fight-Therapy for Divorces" in *Women in Therapy,* edited by Violet Franks and Vasanti Burtle. New York: Brunner/Mazel, 1974.
Bakker, Cornelius B., and Marianne Bakker-Rabdau. *No Trespassing! Explorations in Human Territoriality.* San Francisco: Chandler and Sharp, 1973.
Beck, Aaron T., A. John Rush, Brian F. Shaw, and Gary Emery. *Cognitive Therapy of Depression.* New York: Guilford Press, 1979.
Benson, Herbert. *The Relaxation Response.* New York: Morrow, 1976.
Bergler, Edmund. *Divorce Won't Help.* New York: Harper & Bros., 1948.
Berne, Eric. *Games People Play.* New York: Grove Press, 1964.
Bernstein, Albert. "Handling Angry Customers." Paper Delivered at a Cognitive-Behavioral Seminar, Honolulu, Hawaii, 1985.
Blake, Nelson. *The Road to Reno.* New York: Macmillan, 1962.
Bohannon, Paul S., ed. *Divorce and After.* New York: Doubleday Anchor, 1971.
Cauhape, Elizabeth. *Fresh Starts: Men and Women after Divorce.* New York: Basic Books, 1983.
Coogler, O.J. *Structured Mediation in Divorce Settlement.* Lexington, Mass.: Heath, 1978.
Cull, John G., and Richard E. Hardy. *Deciding on Divorce.* Springfield, Ill.: Charles C. Thomas, 1974.
Douglass, Toni. *Lifers.* Seattle, Washington, 1984. Unpublished.
Ellis, Albert, and Robert A. Harper. *A New Guide to Rational Living.* North Hollywood, Calif.: Wilshire Book Co., 1977.
Emerson, Ralph Waldo. *Essays.* New York: A.L. Burt, 1980.
Erikson, Erik. *Childhood and Society,* 2nd rev. ed. New York: W.W. Norton, 1963.
Franks, Violet, and Vasanti Burtle, Eds. *Women in Therapy.* New York: Bruner/Mazel, 1974.

Goulding, Mary McClure, and Robert L. Goulding. *Changing Lives through Redecision Therapy.* New York: Brunner/Mazel, 1979.
Grollman, Earl A., and Marjorie Sams. *Living through Your Divorce.* Boston: Beacon Press, 1978.
Halem, Lynne Carol. *Divorce Reform.* New York: Free Press, 1980.
Hardy, Richard E., and Cull, John G. *Creative Divorce through Social and Psychological Approaches.* Springfield, Ill.: Charles C Thomas, 1974.
Haynes, John. *Divorce Mediation.* New York: Springer, 1981.
Henry, Carol. Effects of Group Counseling on Divorce Adjustment. doctoral dissertation, University of Washington, Seattle, Wash., 1981.
Holmes, Thomas H., and R.H. Rahe. "The Social Readjustment Rating Scale." *Journal of Psychosomatic Research.* 11 (1967):213–218.
Kessler, Sheila. *The American Way of Divorce: Prescription for Change.* Chicago: Nelson Hall, 1975.
Lederer, William J., and Don D. Jackson. *Mirages of Marriage.* New York: W.W. Norton, 1968.
Levinger, George, and Oliver C. Moles, eds. *Divorce and Separation.* New York: Basic Books, 1979.
Little, Marilyn. *Family Breakup.* San Francisco: Jossey-Bass, 1982.
Loudin, Jo. *The Hoax of Romance.* Englewood Cliffs, N.J.: Prentice-Hall, 1981.
Luther, Martin. *Works,* xxi, edited by Jaroslav Pelikan. St. Louis, MO.: Concordia Publishing House, 1955.
Mahler, Margaret S. *The Selected Papers of Margaret S. Mahler.* New York: Jason Aronson, 1979.
Mattis, Mary. *Sex and the Single Parent.* New York: Henry Holt and Company, 1986.
Milton, John. "Doctrine and Discipline of Divorce" in *Prose Works of John Milton,* edited by R.W. Griswold. Book 1, Chapter 1. Philadelphia: John W. Moore, 1847.
Perls, Fritz. *Gestalt Therapy Verbatim.* Moab, Utah: Real People Press, 1969.
Rice, Joy K., and David G. Rice. *Living through Divorce: A Developmental Approach to Divorce Therapy.* New York: Guilford Press, 1986.
Satir, Virginia. *Conjoint Family Therapy,* 3rd ed. Palo Alto: Science and Behavior Books, 1983.
Schlossberg, Nancy K. *Counseling Adults in Transition.* New York: Springer Publishing Co., 1984.
Sheehy, Gail. *Passages.* New York: Dutton, 1976.
Steiner, Claude. *Scripts People Live.* New York: Grove Press, 1964.
Tavris, Carol. *Anger: The Misunderstood Emotion.* New York: Simon and Schuster, 1982.
Toomin, Marjorie Kawin. "Separation Counseling: A Structured Approach to Marital Crisis" in *Creative Divorce through Social and Psychological Approaches,* edited by Richard Hardy and John G. Cull. Springfield, Ill.: Charles C Thomas, 1974.
Walen, Susan. Lecture on Marriage and Divorce Problems. American Psychological Association Annual Meeting. Los Angeles, Calif. 1983.
Weiss, Robert S. *Marital Separation.* New York: Basic Books, 1975.

Weitzman, Lenore J. *The Divorce Revolution: The Unexpected Social and Economic Consequences for Women and Children in America.* New York: Free Press (Macmillan), 1985.
Zimbardo, Philip G. *Shyness.* Reading, Mass.: Addison-Wesley, 1977.

Self-Help Books

Alberti, Robert E., and Michael L. Emmons. *Your Perfect Right: A Guide to Assertive Behavior,* 4th ed. San Luis Obispo, Calif.: Impact, 1982.
Bach, George R., and Peter Wyden. *The Intimate Enemy.* New York: Morrow, 1968.
Bolles, Richard N. *What Color Is Your Parachute?* Berkeley, Calif.: Ten Speed Press, 1986.
Burns, David. *Feeling Good: The New Mood Therapy.* New York: New American Library (Signet), 1980.
Bryant, Jean. *Playing the Personals.* Kent, Wash.: The Write Idea, 1983.
Cotter, S.B., and J.J. Gruerra. *Assertion Training.* Champaign, Ill.: Research Press, 1976.
Edwards, Marie, and Eleanor Hoover. *The Challenge of Being Single.* New York: Signet, 1975.
Ellis, Albert. *How to Live with and without Anger.* New York: Thomas Y. Crowell, 1977.
Ellis, Albert, and Irving Becker. *A Guide to Personal Happiness.* North Hollywood, Calif.: Wilshire Book Company, 1982.
Fisher, Roger, and William Ury. *Getting to Yes: Negotiating Agreement without Giving In.* New York: Penguin, 1983.
Freidberg, Sidney. "On the Town with the Senior Single." *Modern Maturity* 29 (April-May 1986):98–99.
Gettleman, Susan, and Janet Markowitz. *The Courage to Divorce.* New York: Simon & Schuster, 1974.
Gordon, Thomas. *Parent Effectiveness Training.* New York: Wyden, 1971.
Harris, Thomas A. *I'm O.K., You're O.K.* New York: Harper & Row, 1969.
Hauck, Paul A. *Marriage is a Loving Business.* Philadelphia: Westminster Press, 1977.
Hunt, Morton, and Bernice Hunt. *The Divorce Experience.* Bergenfield, N.J.: New American Library (Signet), 1977.
Jacobson, Edmund. *You Must Relax.* New York: McGraw-Hill, 1976.
James, Muriel, and Dorothy Jongeward. *Born to Win.* New York: Addison-Wesley Publishers, 1971.
Johnson, Stephen M. *First Person Singular: Living the Good Life Alone.* Bergenfield, N.J.: New American Library (Signet), 1977.
Krantzler, Mel. *Creative Divorce.* New York: M. Evans, 1973.
———. *Learning to Love Again.* New York: T.Y. Crowell, 1977.
Lewinsohn, Peter, R. Munoz, and A. Zeiss. *Control Your Depression.* Englewood Cliffs, N.J.: Prentice-Hall, 1978.
McKay, Matthew, Peter D. Rogers, Joan Blades, and Richard Gosse. *The Divorce Book.* Oakland, Calif.: New Harbinger Publications, 1984.

Russianoff, Penelope. *Why Do I Think I Am Nothing Without a Man?* New York: Bantam Books, 1982.
Wanderer, Zev, and Tracy Cabot. *Letting Go.* New York: Warner Books, 1978.
Wassmer, Arthur C. *Making Contact.* New York: Dial, 1978.
Women in Transition, Inc. *Women in Transition: A Feminist Handbook on Separation and Divorce.* New York: Charles Scribner's Sons, 1975.

Books about Parents and Children of Divorce

Cantor, Dorothy W., and Ellen A. Drake. *Divorced Parents and their Children.* New York: Springer Publishing Company, 1983.
Francke, Linda Bird. *Growing up Divorced.* New York: Linden Press/Simon & Schuster, 1983.
Gardner, Richard A. *Psychotherapy with Children of Divorce.* New York: Jason Aronson, 1976.
———. *The Parents Book about Divorce.* New York: Doubleday & Company, 1977.
———. *Family Evaluation in Child Custody Litigation.* Cresskill, N.J.: Creative Therapeutics, 1982.
———. *Child Custody Litigation: A Guide for Parents and Mental Health Professionals.* Cresskill, N.J.: Creative Therapeutics, 1986.
Greif, Geoffrey. *Single Fathers.* Lexington, Mass.: Lexington Books, D.C. Heath, 1985.
Group for the Advancement of Psychiatry. *Divorce, Child Custody and the Family.* San Francisco: Jossey-Bass, Inc. 1980.
Hallett, Kathryn. *A Guide for Single Parents: Transactional Analysis for People in Crisis.* Milbrae: Calif.: Celestial Arts, 1974.
Hetherington, E. Mavis, M. Cox, and R. Cox. "The Aftermath of Divorce" in *Mother-child, Father-child Relations,* edited by J.H. Stevens, Jr., and M. Mathews. Washington, D.C.: National Association for the Education of Young Children, 1978.
Kurdek, Lawrence A. "An Integrative Perspective on Children's Divorce Adjustment." *The American Psychologist.* 36 (August 1981):856–866.
Luepnitz, Deborah Anna. *Child Custody: A Study of Families after Divorce.* Lexington, Mass.: Lexington Books, D.C. Heath, 1982.
Marafiote, Richard. *The Custody of Children: A Behavioral Assessment Model.* New York: Plenum Publishing Company, 1985.
Morawetz, Anita, and Gillian Walker. *Brief Therapy with Single-Parent Families.* New York: Brunner/Mazel, 1984.
Morgenbesser, Mel, and Nadine Nehis. *Joint Custody: An Alternative for Divorcing Families.* Chicago: Nelson Hall, 1981.
Pedro-Carroll, JoAnne L., and Emory L. Cowen. "The Children of Divorce Intervention Program: An Investigation of the Efficacy of a School-Based Prevention Program." *Journal of Consulting and Clinical Psychology.* 53 (October 1985): 603–611.

Ricci, Isolina. *Mom's House, Dad's House: Making Shared Custody Work.* New York: Macmillan, 1980.
Roman, Melvin, and William Haddad. *The Disposable Parent.* New York: Holt, Rinehart and Winston, 1978.
Tessman, Lora H. *Children of Parting Parents.* New York: Jason Aronson, 1978.
Stuart, Irving R., and Lawrence Edwin Abt, eds. *Children of Separation and Divorce.* Florence, Ky.: Van Nostrand Reinhold, 1981.
Wallerstein, Judith, and Joan Kelly. *Surviving the Breakup: How Parents and Children Cope with Divorce.* New York: Basic Books, 1980.
Weiss, Robert S. *Going it Alone: The Family Life and Social Situation of the Single Parent.* New York: Basic Books, 1979.

Books about Stepfamilies

Furstenberg, Frank F., and Graham B. Spanier. *Recycling the Family: Remarriage after Divorce.* Beverly Hills, Calif.: Sage Publications, 1984.
Mowatt, Marian. "Group Psychotherapy for Stepfathers and their Wives," *Psychotherapy: Theory, Research and Practice.* 9 (Winter 1972):328–331.
Sager, Clifford, H.S. Brown, H. Crohn, T. Engel, E. Rodstein, and L. Walker. *Treating the Remarried Family.* New York: Brunner/Mazel, 1983.
Stuart, Richard B., and Barbara Jacobson. *Second Marriage.* New York: W.W. Norton, 1985.
Visher, Emily, and John Visher. *How to Win as a Stepfamily.* New York: December Books, 1982.
———. *Stepfamilies: A Guide to Working with Stepparents and Stepchildren.* New York: Brunner/Mazel, 1979.
Wald, Esther. *The Remarried Family: Challenge and Promise.* New York: Family Service Association Publications, 1981.

Books for Children of Divorce

Adams, Florence. *Mushy Eggs.* New York: Putnam and Sons, 1973. (For ages 5–10.)
Anderson, Hal, and Gail S. Anderson. *Mom and Dad Are Divorced, but I'm Not.* Chicago: Nelson Hall, 1981.
Bienfeld, Florence. *My Mom and Dad Are Getting a Divorce.* St. Paul, Minn.: EMC, 1980.
Blume, Judy. *It's Not the End of the World.* New York: Bantam Books, 1972. (For ages 8 and up.)
Gardner, Richard A. *The Boys and Girls Book about Divorce.* New York: Jason Aronson, 1970. (For ages 8 and up.)
———. *The Boys and Girls Book about Stepfamilies.* New York: Bantam Books, 1982.
Hazen, Barbara Shook. *Two Homes to Live in: A Child's Eye View of Divorce.* New York: Human Sciences Press, 1978. (Ages 4–8.)

LeShan, Eda. *What's Going to Happen to Me?* New York: Four Winds Press, 1978.
Richards, Arlene, and Irene Willis. *How to Get it Together when your Parents Are Coming Apart.* New York: Bantam Books, 1977. (For adolescents.)
Salk, Lee. *What Every Child Would Like Parents to Know about Divorce.* New York: Warner, 1979.

Periodicals

The Journal of Divorce. New York: Haworth Press.
Marriage and Divorce Today Newsletter. New York: ATCOM, Inc.
The Single Parent. c/o Parents without Partners. Washington, D.C.

Psychological Tests

Beck Depression Inventory in *Depression,* Aaron T. Beck. New York: Harper and Row, 1967.
Career Assessment Inventory. Charles B. Johansson. Minneapolis, Minn.: National Computer Systems, 1976.
Kinetic Family Drawings (KFD). Robert C. Burns and S. Harvard Kaufman. New York: Brunner/Mazel, 1970.
Minnesota Multiphasic Personality Inventory. S.R. Hathaway and J.C. McKinley. Minneapolis, Minn.: National Computer Systems, 1976.
Rokeach Values Survey in *The Nature of Human Values*, Milton Rokeach. New York: Free Press, 1973.
Strong-Campbell Interest Inventory. Edward K. Strong, Jr., and David P. Campbell. Palo Alto, Calif.: Consulting Psychologists Press, 1974.
Zung Self-Rating Depression Scale in *The Measurement of Depression,* William W.K. Zung. Columbus, Ohio: Merrill, 1975.

Index

Abusive behavior, 14
Adolescents: effect of divorce on, 101–102; and parent's sexuality, 65
Aid to Families with Dependent Children, 35, 46, 103, 143
Alcoholism, 7, 14, 71, 130
Alimony, 46
Anger, 17, 18, 21; characteristics of, 89–90; fear of, 91, 93; learned ways of expressing, 91, 98; methods for alleviating, 92; positive value of, 90
Anxiety, 18, 76
Appreciation, 114, 137
Assertiveness, 76, 96, 144
Attachment, need for, 83–84
Attitude: toward divorce, 1–2; toward marital problems, 14
Attorneys: 51, as adversaries, 89
Autonomy, 125

Babysitters, 48, 115
Battered women, 34, 84, 90, 130–131
Beliefs: irrational beliefs, 77, 78

Career Assessment Inventory, 125
Career counseling, 47, 50, 68–69, 125
Changes: effect of, on marriage, 23–26; changes within a marriage, 15, 24, 33–34; willingness to change, 15, 23, 24–25
Child support, 35, 45–46, 51, 68, 143; and missing payments, 46; and relationship to visitations, 111
Children, behavior after visitation, 109; behavior problems in, 113–116; and custody arrangements, 102–107; effect of divorce on self-esteem, 108; effect of first child on marriage, 27; explaining divorce to, 107–108; handicapped, as factor in marital disruption, 27; interviewing, in custody disputes, 105–106; and parent's sexuality, 64–66; and psychological effects of divorce, 101–102; and remarriage, 132; and visitation arrangements, 108–112; and wish for parents' reconciliation, 102
Cognitive method of therapy, 43, 57, 76, 78–79, 124–125
Communication, between divorced parents, 101; between parents and children, 65, 112; in remarriage, 140; role of poor communication in divorce, 16–17
Competition: effect of, on marital relationship, 131
Conflict: areas of, in marriage, 14; escalation of, 94–95; learning to handle, 95–99, 136, 144
Control. *See* Need to control
Counseling: assessing the client's marriage, 13–30; and counselors' biases, 11, 121, 125; on decision to divorce, 9–30; and first interview, 12–14; postdivorce counseling, 119–127; premarital counseling, 129; and stepparenting, 137–141; and values clarification before remarriage, 131–132. *See also* Career counseling
Court battles, 105, 106
Custodial parent, 46
Custody, 102–108; conflicts in, 31,

Custody (*continued*)
89, 105; father as custodial parent, 102–103; joint custody, 103–104; mother as custodial parent, 103; mother as noncustodial parent, 116–117; uniform child custody laws, 146

Dating, 60, 61, 62; dating services, 122
Daycare centers, 46, 116, 118
Decision to divorce: and assessing the marriage, 13–30; difficulty of, 9–30; exercises to aid in, 28–29; and solving practical problems, 45–54
Dependency needs, 37, 39, 82, 84, 130
Depression: assessing the seriousness of, 74–75; and cognitive method of therapy, 78–80; dealing with, 73–87; and dysfunctional behavior, 75–78; and earlier loss, 82; and guilt feelings, 86–87; ideas leading to, 73; and obsessive thinking, 83–86; and unrealistic demands, 78–80
Desensitization, 63, 68
Displaced Homemaker program, 47, 120, 125, 146
Dissolution. *See* Divorce
Divorce: and accident rate, 7; adjustment after divorce, 119–127; and alcoholism, 7; contemporary attitudes toward, 5–6, 7; cost of, to society, 143; counseling on decision to, 9–30; and counselors' attitudes toward, 1–2, 4–6, 7; as "failure," 56–57, 78; grounds for, 2–5; history of, 2–5, 7; lack of rituals surrounding, 56; and mental illness, 6–7; and mortality rate, 7; no-fault divorce, 5; practical problems of, 45–54; and effects on children, 101–102; reasons for avoiding, 34–35, 52–53; and remarriage rate, 5; stages of, 119; and suicide, 7
Divorce ceremony, 43
Divorce classes, 47;
Divorce etiquette, 59
Divorce insurance, 146
Do-it-yourself divorce, 51

Ego states: parent-adult-child model, 20, 37–38, 88; adult, 20, 23, 86, 92, 95; child, 20, 92, 95; parent, 20, 23, 63
Emotions: and behavior problems in children after divorce, 113–116; children's feelings after divorce, 113–116; children's feelings after visitation, 109–110; and depression, 73, after divorce, 13, 119–127; effect of suppressing, 93; escalation of, 89; positive feelings, 137; rage and revenge, 89–99. *See also* Guilt
Expectations: about love and sexuality, 19–20; in marriage, 14–15, 24, 135

Family: reactions of, to divorced person, 57; as support group, 115
Father: as custodial parent, 102–103, 116
Fathers' rights organizations, 112
Fears: and avoiding divorce, 34–41, 52–53; of being alone, 37, 38, 82; of change, 43; of hurting parents, 36; of rejection, 63, 123
Feelings, 17–18. *See also* Emotions
Financial problems, 14, 26–27, 35, 48–49; after divorce, 45–47
Friends: reaction to divorce, 60
Frustration tolerance, 14, 134

Games (Berne's), 36, 52, 80, 98, 123
Gender differences: and assuming new roles after divorce, 65–68, 135; and depression, 74; role of, in divorce, 11–12; and sexuality, 19
"Good guy" image, 22, 36
Grandparents: relationship with grandchildren after divorce, 58–59
Group therapy: value of, in divorce counseling, 27, 47–48, 51–54, 60–61
Guilt, 21, 27, 39–40, 86–87; guilt feelings of parents, 69, 113–114; relieving guilt feelings, 40–41; and sex outside of marriage, 64; and value of appropriate guilt, 87
Guilt induction: as expression of anger, 98

Head of household: as new role for men, 65–66; as new role for women, 66–68

Homosexuality, 64, 140
Housework, 136
Housing arrangements, 45, 49–50; after divorce, 69–70

Identity, sense of, 55, 56, 71
Indifference, 136
Inferiority complex, 81
Infidelity, 14; counselors' attitudes toward, 20; meaning of, to marital partners, 20–21; reasons for, 21–23
In-laws: relationship with former, 57–58
Intimacy, 21, 22

Jealousy, 133, 137–138
Job training: for women after divorce, 46, 70. See also Career counseling
Joint custody, 103–104

Kidnapping, 35, 117–118
Kinetic Family Drawing, 105

"Latch-key children," 115, 116
Laws: uniform child custody laws, 146; uniform divorce laws, 146
Legal services, low-cost, 35
Leisure activities, 120
Letting go, 85
Life script, 55, 80–83
Living alone, 127
Living together without marrying, 5–6, 129, 140; and child custody, 107, and decision to separate, 42
Loneliness, 73
Love, 10, 17, 19, 135, 138
Love versus attachment, 84

Maintenance, 46–47
Marriage: education for, 143–144; factors in lasting marriages, 6; futile attempts to save, 92; nurturing of, 135; parental marriage as model, 14–15; preventing inappropriate marriages, 144. See also Remarriage
Marriage insurance, 146
Mediation, 51, 98, 99, 145, 146
Men: and acceptance of new, single role, 61; economic effects of divorce on, 45–46; and fears of rejection, 124–125; as head of household, 65–66; and reasons for avoiding divorce, 34; and remarriage, 126;
and suicide, 74. See also Gender differences
Mental illness, 6–7
Money: as cause of marital disruption, 26–27; ways of making, 49–50. See also Financial problems
Mother: as noncustodial parent, 116–117

National Congress for Men, 145
National Organization for Women, 145
Need to control, 16, 23, 28, 66, 111
Negative feelings: See Emotions
No-fault divorce, 5, 89
Noncustodial parent, 101, 112, 116–117; and remarriage, 139–140
Nurturing, 135

Obsessive thoughts, 83–86

Parent injunctions, 37–38
Parents Without Partners, 64, 91, 126, 144
Personality traits, 14, 144; and choosing mates, 25–26; as factor in divorce, 23–26; and remarriage, 133
Positive reinforcement, 34, 75–76, 114, 137, 140; defined, 10
Psychological evaluation: for child custody, 105
Psychological tests: for depression after divorce, 74, 121; premarital, 132
Punishment, 114, 140–141

Rational-emotive method of therapy, 16, 37–38, 92, 119–120
Reconciliation: as wish of children of divorce, 102
Reinforcement. See Positive reinforcement
Relaxation techniques, 71, 76
Religious beliefs: as rationalization for fears, 41; as reason to avoid divorce, 41
Religious differences: as factor in marital disruption, 27
Remarriage: and clarification of values, 131–132; and conflict management, 135–136; hasty, 64, 71, 129, 130; making better choices in, 129–134; and stepparenting, 137–141

Rescuer role, 36, 38–39, 40, 130
Revenge, 111; in custody disputes, 106; fantasies of, 93–95
Role changes: accepting new roles, 60–61; assuming new sexual roles, 62–65; assuming the single role, 60–66; within the family, 57–59; as single head of household, 65–68; in social network, 59–60; stress of multiple role changes, 55–71; wage earner role, 69
Role playing, 67, 68–69, 76, 124
Romance, fading of, 10–11; and relationship to marriage, 9–10, 17

Self-acceptance, 12
Self-blame, 73, 77, 78
Self-confidence, 65, 114, 125, 126, 130
Self-esteem, 15, 55, 62, 76, 110, 136
Self-image, 55, 56, 57, 67, 81, 121
Separation: creative, 29; structured, 28–29
Setting limits, 65, 114
Sex: fear of discussing, 63–64; outside of marriage, 64
Sex education, 143–144
Sexual problems, 19–20; as symptom of marital problem, 19–20
Sexuality, 19–23; and remarriage, 132
"Shoulds," 37–38, 39, 79, 135; and marital expectations, 14–15
Shyness, 124–125
Single parents, 69, 144
Singleness (being single), 121–126
Singles organizations, 144
Social network, 120; changes in, for divorced person, 59–60
Social Readjustment Rating Scale, 70
Social relationships, in depression, 76

Social skills, 125
Stepparenting, 137–141
Stress: of multiple role changes, 70–71
Stress management, 71
Stress tolerance, 56
Strong-Campbell Interest Inventory, 125
Suicide, 7, 40, 74
Support group, 61–62

Taking responsibility for one's own actions, 40, 43
The Values Survey, 132
Thinking: all-or-nothing thinking, 77
Thought-stopping, 84–85, 95
"Top dog" versus "underdog": attitude in marriage, 16, 28
Transactional analysis, 80–83; use of, in marital counseling, 20, 23, 35–37
Trust, 12, 16, 26–27

Values, 43, 131; clarification of, in marriage, 32–33; in remarriage, 131–132
Victim role, 35, 38–39, 40, 69, 80, 86, 90, 114; payoffs in, 36
Victim-rescuer-persecutor triangle, 35–36, 80, 86, 130
Visitation, 51, 59, 89, 108–112

Women: and acceptance of new, single role, 61–62; and drop in standard of living after divorce, 45–47; as head of household, 66–68; and name change after divorce, 56; and new wage earner role, 69; and reasons for avoiding divorce, 34, 52–53; and remarriage, 126; and suicide, 74; and support groups, 61–62. *See also* Gender differences

About the Author

Marian Mowatt is a clinical psychologist in private practice in Seattle and an auxiliary faculty member at the University of Washington. She has taught at several colleges and is a consultant to social agencies in the Seattle area. She received her B.A. degree in social sciences at Swarthmore College and her Ph.D. degree in psychology from Bryn Mawr College. She counsels couples and individuals including many people in the midst of dissolution. These clients, as well as Dr. Mowatt's experience with divorce and raising two children as a single parent have contributed to her knowledge of the subject.

N

D